Bean Cooking

Linda Turner and Diane Newsom

First published in 2014 by New Holland Publishers Pty Ltd
London • Sydney • Cape Town • Auckland

The Chandlery Unit 114 50 Westminster Bridge Road London SE1 7QY United Kingdom
1/66 Gibbes Street Chatswood NSW 2067 Australia
Wembley Square First Floor Solan Road Gardens Cape Town 8001 South Africa
218 Lake Road Northcote Auckland New Zealand

www.newhollandpublishers.com

A record of this book is held at the British Library and the National Library of Australia.

ISBN 9781742574905

Managing director: Fiona Schultz
Publisher: Linda Williams
Project Editor: Jodi De Vantier
Designer: Tracy Loughlin
Photographs: Sue Stubbs
Food stylist: Tracy Rutherford
Production director: Olga Dementiev
Printer: Toppan Leefung Printing Ltd (China)

10 9 8 7 6 5 4 3 2 1

Keep up with New Holland Publishers on Facebook
www.facebook.com/NewHollandPublishers

Bean Cooking

Linda Turner and Diane Newsom

NEW HOLLAND

Contents

Introduction

Linda Turner and Diane Newsom have 'bean cooking' in various kitchens commercially and domestically for many years and thought it was time to share some of their favourite bean by name recipes. Often neglected in modern cuisine, beans are nutritious and wonderfully versatile as they can be included in so many recipes to add colour, texture and flavour.

You may wonder how Linda and Diane could come up with 80 individual recipes for *Bean Cooking*. However, once they started listing recipes using Green, Broad, Soy, Borlotti, Red, Black, Butter, Bean Sprouts, Coffee and Vanilla Beans, to mention but a few with bean in their name, they realised that they had better stop thinking and start cooking.

The family of beans is very broad with some being vegetables or fruits and the majority being pulses which are part of the legume family of plants. When growing, pulses fix nitrogen into the soil, reducing the need for chemical fertilizers, an excellent environmental outcome for us all. Pulses also have significant nutritional and health advantages.

As if we could leave out one of the world's most loved 'beans'—coffee!

I am an 'open a jar' sort of person but it has to be a good quality one—Di is a smooth good quality machine coffee girl. We are going to feature cooking with coffee in a couple of recipes just to show the diversity of this 'bean'.

You then have fruits like vanilla beans that can be used in amazing desserts and bean sprouts that are just lucky enough to have bean in their name . So many beans not enough time as the saying goes.

This book will make your family and guests sit up and take notice of how creative and ingenious you are, producing great looking and tasting meals that readily fit the family budget. Once you delve into the extensive range of beans by name available and their adaptability, you will love every minute of cooking and eating the results.

Beans and other pulses are packed with significant health benefits. Pulses are 20 to 25 per cent protein by weight, which is double the protein content of wheat and three times that of rice.

They are a great source of soluble fibre that helps to lower cholesterol and insoluble fibre that is important for bowel health. Together they help to reduce the risk of heart disease and diabetes.

Beans are also a low-fat carbohydrate and protein source, with high levels of minerals such as iron, zinc, phosphorous, magnesium and calcium, as well as folate and other B-vitamins. Beans have a low glycaemic index which means they can help you feel full for longer.

Cooking Methods for Dried Beans

There are so many ways to prepare beans especially if you happen to buy them dried instead of ready-to-use cans or, of course, fresh.

The Quick Method requires placing 1 cup of beans in a saucepan and covering with 3 cups of water. Bring it to the boil and then simmer them for approximately 60 minutes until they are tender. Sometimes you have to skim off the foam while they are simmering.

The Traditional Method is soaking the beans for approximately 6 to 8 hours. You then drain and refill the saucepan with fresh water bring it to the boil and cook for approximately 30 minutes.

Some Basic Hints

Any amount of soaking will reduce the cooking times stated in recipes so do not worry if you are opening a can or a packet.

Depending on the age of the beans the cooking times will vary. Packaging usually won't tell you when beans have been picked and packed, so testing a small batch before using is vital.

After cooking your beans don't throw away the water—it makes a great stock for soups and sauces.

Beans can be frozen for up to 6 months and still retain their nutrition so do not worry if you have left overs; pop them in the freezer, well labelled, until you are ready for the next exciting bean recipe.

There is also a magic way to make your house smell beautiful especially after cooking cabbage or chilli con carne. Boil a saucepan of water, add lemon slices, couple sprigs of rosemary and 2 teaspoons of vanilla and your house becomes the flavour of spring!

Bean Cooking has something for everyone including vegetarian, meat and seafood recipes. These include Zucchini, Broad Bean and Ricotta Bruschetta to start; Greek Style Lamb & Bean Soup to

follow; then salads with flavours from Asia, India, Mexico and Aussie modern cuisine; mains such as Baked Salmon Fillet with Broad Beans; and desserts such as Coffee and Raspberry Ice-cream and Vanilla Biscuits. The diverse range of recipes is sure to please everyone in the family and will definitely satisfy their taste buds.

While including tasty vegetarian recipes that acknowledge the importance of beans by name, in both their raw and cooked states, as staples in vegetarian diets, we have also provided some meaty carnivore and salty seafood recipes. *Bean Cooking* has something for everyone. So come on our journey and enjoy the world of bean cooking!

DIPS AND ENTREES

Chicken and Bean Sprouts Sang Choy Bau

Serves: 6 / Preparation: 20 mins / Cooking time: 13 mins

1 head iceberg lettuce

1 tablespoon olive oil

3 scallions (spring onions), thinly sliced
  diagonally

1 clove garlic, crushed

17½ oz (500 g) ground (minced) chicken

1 small carrot, peeled, grated

1 zucchini (courgette), grated

1 small red bell pepper (capsicum),
  deseeded, finely diced

4 oz (125 g) can corn kernels, drained

7 oz (200 g) bean sprouts

⅓ cup oyster sauce

¼ cup tomato sauce

With the core of the lettuce facing down, bang core on a flat surface. This will make it easy to remove whole core by twisting and pulling out. Remove damaged outer leaves and discard.

Separate leaves and place in a large bowl of icy cold water. Refrigerate until required.

Heat oil in a frying pan over medium heat. Add scallions and garlic. Cook for 1 minute. Increase heat to high. Add chicken mince. Cook, stirring, for 4 minutes or until browned. Add carrot, zucchini, bell pepper and corn. Stir well. Combine oyster sauce and tomato sauce in a jug. Add to chicken mince mixture. Stir well. Bring to the boil. Reduce heat. Simmer for 2 minutes.

Turn off heat and stir bean sprouts through the mixture

Remove lettuce leaves from bowl. Pat dry with paper towel. Place lettuce cups on a platter. Spoon mince mixture into lettuce cups.

Serve. You can also replace the corn with 8 oz (230 g) can of water chestnuts. They are a little more expensive but add crunch.

Heirloom Tomato and Bean Salsa

1 x 14 oz (400 g) can five-bean mix, drained and rinsed

1 punnet heirloom tomatoes, cut in half

1 small red onion, thinly sliced

1 large chilli, seeds removed and finely chopped

1 tablespoon chopped cilantro (coriander)

2 tablespoons lime juice

salt and pepper, to taste

Combine beans, tomatoes, onion, chilli, coriander and lime juice in medium bowl. Season with salt and pepper.

Cover and let the dish stand at room temperature for 1 hour before serving to allow the flavours to blend.

Salsa is a great side dish to serve with fish or chicken or as a snack with corn chips.

Green Beans, Rocket and Nut Salad

2½ oz (75 g) macadamia or brazil nuts
1 lb (500 g) green beans, topped and tailed
2½ oz (80 g) parmesan, shaved
9 oz (250 g) arugula (rocket)

DRESSING
2½ fl oz (80 ml) macadamia oil or any nut-
   flavoured oil

2 fl oz (60 ml) orange juice, no pith
1 tablespoon crunchy peanut butter
1 tablespoon white vinegar
1 clove garlic, crushed
cracked black pepper, to taste

Line a roasting tray with baking paper, spread over the macadamia nuts and roast in hot oven for 3 minutes until golden brown. Chop roughly when cool.

In a medium-size saucepan, bring water to the boil, add green beans and cook for 1 minute. Drain and refresh beans in cold water to retain their colour.

To make the dressing, place all ingredients into a blender or food processor and combine.

Place green beans and rocket in bowl and toss with dressing. Transfer to serving platter and scatter with parmesan and chopped macadamia nuts (or nuts to match the oil you are using). Season with ground black pepper to taste.

Smoked Trout and Broad Bean Tart

 Serves 4 / Preparation: 60 mins / Total cooking time: 60 mins

6 oz (170 g) all-purpose (plain) flour
2½ oz (75 g) chilled unsalted butter, chopped
salt and pepper
10½ oz (300 g) fresh or frozen broad beans
    (podded)
1 x 4 oz (125 g) smoked trout, flaked
10 cherry or grape tomatoes, cut in half
5½ oz (160 g) feta cheese, break into chunks
2 eggs, lightly beaten

4 fl oz (125 ml) pure thin cream,
fresh dill, for serving
extra virgin olive oil, to drizzle

Whiz the flour, butter and a pinch of salt in a food processor until it resembles fine breadcrumbs. Add up to 3 tablespoons cold water and pulse until dough just comes together.

Remove and shape into a ball. Wrap in cling wrap and chill for 20 minutes.

Preheat the oven to 400°F (200°C). Roll the chilled pastry on a lightly floured board to fit a 9½ in (24 cm) loose-bottomed tart pan. Chill for 15 minutes.

Line the pastry with baking paper and fill with pastry weights or uncooked rice. Bake on a tray in the oven for 15 minutes. Remove weights and paper and bake for a further 15 minutes or until golden.

Meanwhile, blanch fresh beans in boiling salted water for 2–3 minutes. Rinse in cold water, then remove skins, i.e., pod. Arrange trout, beans, tomatoes and 3½ oz (100 g) feta in the tart case. Beat the eggs and cream together and season with salt and pepper. Pour the egg mixture into the tart shell. Bake for 20–25 minutes at 180°C or until just set. Cool for 10 minutes and then remove from pan. Cut into 4 pieces.

Serve, topped with remaining feta cheese, fresh dill and a drizzle of olive oil.

Lima Bean and Tuna Bake

Serves 6 / Preparation: 30 mins (excludes lima bean cooking time) / Cooking time: 25 mins

6 oz (185 g) dried lima beans
1 clove garlic, crushed
2 oz (60 g) butter, softened
6 oz (180 g) chilli-infused tuna in oil
¾ cup cheddar cheese, grated

2 tablespoons parsley, finely chopped
zest of 1 lemon
sea salt and pepper, to taste
¼ cup breadcrumbs (fresh if possible)

Place the lima beans and 3 cups of water into a saucepan and bring to the boil. Simmer for approximately 45 minutes or until the beans are soft.

Preheat the oven to 350°F (180°C).

When cooked, puree the beans, garlic and half the butter in a blender. Place in a bowl.

Stir through tuna, cheese, parsley and lemon zest and season to taste.

Press mixture into a lightly buttered three-cup capacity ovenproof bowl. Sprinkle evenly with breadcrumbs and dot with remaining butter. Bake for 25 minutes or until breadcrumbs have browned. Serve warm.

This mixture also works as a stuffing for mushrooms.

Mini Lamb Taco Shells

Serves 8 / Preparation time: 15 mins / Cooking time: 30 mins

 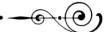

2 tablespoons olive oil
2 medium onions, thinly sliced
4 cloves garlic, chopped
1 teaspoon cumin seeds
1 heaped tablespoon ground cumin
2 tablespoons tomato paste
1 lb 2oz (500 g) ground (minced) lamb
1 x 14 oz (400 g) can cannellini beans,
    drained, washed and lightly smashed

1 tablespoon soy sauce
¼ teaspoon chilli powder
1 cup hot water
1 cup frozen peas
1 pkt taco shells
1–2 chillies, finely chopped
lime wedges, to serve

Heat the olive oil in a deep frying pan. Add onions and cook until soft. Stir in the garlic, cumin seeds, ground cumin and tomatoe paste, cook for a further 1–2 minutes until fragrant. Add the mince and cook until browned. Add smashed white beans, soy sauce, chilli powder and water.

Stir, cover and simmer on low heat for 10 minutes. Watch that there is enough liquid in the pan and add some more if it has evaporated. Stir in the frozen peas and cook for another 8 minutes.

When you add the peas to the mixture, place the taco shells on an ovenproof tray lined with baking paper. Heat as per instructions on the box they come in.

When ready to serve, place a small amount of lamb mixture in each taco and place on a tray or a deep glass dish. Garnish with red chillies and lime wedges.

Chilli Con Carne Pockets

I quantity Chilli Con Carne (see recipe
page 88)

POCKET INGREDIENTS
12 bread slices, trimmed of all crusts

1¾ oz (50 g) butter plus extra butter to
grease the muffin tray
sour cream, to serve
scallions (spring onions), finely chopped, for
garnish
dried chillies, for garnish

Preheat the oven to 400°F (200°C).

Heat the prepared chilli con carne through. You can add some chopped jalapenos if you like it a little hotter to taste.

Butter both sides of the bread slices. Grease the muffin tin. Press the slices firmly into the tin. Place the tin into the hot oven for 8 minutes until crisp and toasted.

Remove them from the tin and place on cooling rack. When cool, spoon chilli con carne mixture in pockets. Place on a tray with baking paper and reheat before serving approximately 4 minutes.

Garnish with a dollop of sour cream, some chopped scallions and a sprinkle of chilli.

Stuffed Peppers with White Beans

Serves 4 / Preparation: 15 mins / Total cooking time: 25 mins

4 red bell peppers (capsicums)
4 bacon rashers, cut into thin slices
2 cloves garlic, finely chopped
1 onion, finely chopped
2 stalks celery, finely chopped
1 x 400 g (14 oz) can cannellini beans, rinsed and drained

2 teaspoons fresh thyme leaves
1 tablespoon olive oil
pepper and salt
arugula (rocket) leaves, to serve
¼ cup pine nuts, toasted
juice of 1 lemon

Preheat oven to 480°F (250°C). Place whole peppers upright on baking tray lined with baking paper. Cover stalks with foil to prevent burning. Roast for 15 minutes or until skin blisters and turns black and the flesh has softened. Reduce the oven temperature to 400°F (200°C).

Remove the peppers from the oven, wrap in cling wrap for 5 minutes to sweat, then peel. With a sharp knife, carefully cut a 1 in (2 cm) lid on the top of the peppers, then scoop out and discard the membrane, seeds and liquid.

Cook bacon in a non-stick pan over a medium heat for about 2 minutes, stirring constantly until it starts to brown. Add garlic, onion and celery and stir for 3 minutes or until mixture softens. Add drained beans, thyme and oil and cook for 1 minute. Remove pan from heat, season with pepper and salt to taste.

Place peppers back on baking tray, fill with the bean mixture (about ⅔ cup for each one), then pop on lids. Return stuffed peppers to the oven and cook for 5 minutes. Remove the foil from stem.

Serve with rocket leaves scattered with pine nuts and a squeeze of lemon juice.

White Bean and Ham Pattie with Dill Sauce

Serves 4 / Preparation: 30 mins / Total cooking time: 20 mins

olive oil, to shallow fry
1 onion, finely chopped
12 oz (350 g) leg ham
1 x 14 oz (400 g) can cannellini beans,
    drained and rinsed
2 cloves garlic, finely chopped
2 tablespoons flat-leaf parsley
2 teaspoons Dijon mustard
5 oz (150 g) all-purpose (plain) flour
2 eggs, lightly beaten

14 oz (400 g) breadcrumbs
lemon wedges, to serve
mixed green salad, to serve

DILL SAUCE
½ cup sour cream
1½ teaspoons Dijon mustard
1 tablespoon lemon juice
2 teaspoons fresh dill, chopped

Heat one tablespoon of oil in a frying pan over medium heat. Cook the onion for 2–3 minutes until softened, not browned. Cool slightly.

Roughly chop ham in a food processor, then add the beans, garlic, parsley, mustard and onion. Pulse until you have a coarse patty mixture, then form into 12 small round patties, about 3 in (6 cm) across. Chill for 15 minutes.

Place flour, egg and breadcrumbs separately in three shallow dishes. Dip each patty first in flour, then egg, followed by breadcrumbs.

Heat 1 in (2 cm) oil in a large frying pan over medium to high heat. In two batches, cook patties for two to three minutes each side until crisp and golden.

Serve on a platter with lemon wedges and salad accompanied by the Dill Sauce.

DILL SAUCE
Mix with a whisk until well blended. Chill for approximately 30 minutes before serving.

Edamame Chilli Lime Beans

 Serves 4 / Preparation: 10 mins / Total cooking time: 25 mins

7 oz (200 g) frozen soybeans (also known as
   edamame)
2 tablespoons chilli-lime salt (see recipe
   below)

CHILLI LIME SALT
½ cup salt flakes
1 teaspoon chilli flakes
½ teaspoon dried lime rind

Cook beans in a pan of boiling water for 2 minutes. Drain and refresh under cold water.

When cool, place beans in a serving bowl with chilli-lime salt and toss to coat.

To make a basic chilli lime salt, mix together the ingredients in a blender or spice grinder until you have a powder. Place in an air-tight jar. This will last up to 3 months in a cool pantry.

Broad Bean and Feta Dip

1½ cups broad beans, podded

4 oz (125 g) ricotta cheese

1¾ oz (50 g) feta

¼ cup light sour cream

2 cloves garlic, minced

1 teaspoon chilli, minced

2 teaspoons lemon juice

freshly ground black pepper

pinch of salt

1 bunch mini asparagus, trimmed

Blanch the broad beans in boiling salted water for about 3 minutes until tender. Remove skins, i.e., pod.

Blanch asparagus in hot water and refresh in cold water.

In a blender, add the beans, ricotta cheese, feta, sour cream, garlic, chilli and lemon juice and blend until you have a smooth consistency.

Place dip in a bowl, season with salt and pepper and decorate with mini asparagus.

This dip is delicious with cut raw vegetables and pieces of crusty sourdough bread.

Zucchini, Broad Bean and Pea Bruschetta

Serves 4–6, depending on thickness of slices / Preparation: 20 mins / Total cooking time: 15 mins

3 medium zucchini (courgette), halved
    lengthways
1 medium lemon, juice and zest
2 cloves garlic, crushed
3 tablespoons extra virgin olive oil, plus extra
    to drizzle
cracked pepper and rock salt

7 oz (200 g) frozen broad beans
7 oz (200 g) 200 g frozen peas
½ bunch fresh mint, roughly chopped
10 slices crusty bread
1 garlic clove, halved
10½ oz (300 g) fresh ricotta

Heat griddle or barbecue to hot. Cook halved zucchini lengths for 1–2 minutes each side or until charred. Cut into 1 in (2–3 cm) rough slices then toss in a bowl with lemon juice, garlic, extra virgin olive oil, pepper and salt. Leave to cool.

Cook broad beans in a saucepan of boiling water for 2 minutes, add peas and cook for a further 2 minutes, drain and refresh under cold water.

Toss beans and peas into bowl with zucchini and gently mix through chopped mint.

Cook sliced bread on griddle or barbecue on both sides. Rub one side with the halved garlic and top with ricotta and the lemon zest. Drizzle with extra virgin olive oil and pile zucchini mix on top.

This dish can be served as an entree or with a green salad for lunch.

Beans, Chilli and Garlic Swirls

Makes 12 / Preparation: 8 mins / Total cooking time: 25 mins

1 x 14 oz (400 g) can cannellini beans,
    drained and rinsed
2 teaspoons finely chopped chilli
2 teaspoons garlic, finely chopped
2 tablespoons butter, softened
1 egg, lightly beaten
12 pieces shaved parmesan

COFFEE BARBECUE DIPPING SAUCE
1 teaspoon coffee granules (good quality)
½ cup water
¼ cup worstershire cauce (or tamari)
¼ cup brown sugar
1 oz (30 g) butter, softened
½ cup tomato passata
2 tablespoons brown vinegar
2 tablespoons lemon juice

Preheat the oven to 400°F (200°C).

Place the beans in a blender. Add the chilli, garlic, butter and beaten egg.

Blend on high for approximately 2 minutes until fine and smooth.

Line a baking tray with baking paper. Place the mixture in a piping bag and make approximately 12 swirls on the tray. If you don't have a piping bag, just use a spoon to dollop on the mixture. Place a flake of parmesan cheese on each swirl.

Bake in the oven for about 25 minutes or until golden.

To make the Coffee Barbeque Dipping Sauce, combine all ingredients in a small saucepan. Bring to the boil and simmer over medium heat for 5 minutes until all ingredients are blended. Remove from the heat and allow to cool before serving.

Serve the swirls with the dipping sauce.

These snacks are party favourites and have a bit of a kick to them.

Quick Three Bean Dip

Serves 6 / Preparation time: 10 mins / Cooking time: 2 mins

1 x 14 oz (400 g) can three-bean mix, drained
  and rinsed
1 clove garlic, grated
zest of 1 lemon
½ lemon, juice

⅓ cup olive oil
salt and ground pepper
2 tablespoons chopped flat-leaf parsley
1 tablespoon chopped chives

Combine beans, garlic, lemon zest and half the lemon juice in a small food processor. Process until finely blended. While the motor is running, pour a fine stream of olive oil into the mixture. Process until creamy.

Add more lemon juice to taste if needed.

Transfer ingredients to a serving bowl and season with salt and ground pepper. Stir through parsley and chives.

This dip makes a wonderful addition to an appetizer platter. Serve with zucchini, carrot and celery stalks or bread sticks.

Summer Bean Dip

Preparation time: 20 mins

1 large avocado, mashed
¼ teaspoon lemon juice
1 x 14 oz (400g) can red kidney beans,
   drained and rinsed
1 x 9 oz (250 g) tub sour cream (Greek yogurt
   can be substituted)

9 oz (250 g) store-bought tomato salsa
3 large roma tomatoes, roughly chopped
½ bunch scallions (shallots), roughly chopped
2 cups grated cheddar cheese
¼ cup parmesan shavings

Mash the avocado and the lemon juice in the bottom of your chosen serving bowl. Using a large glass dish will show the layers off to full effect.

Mash the red kidney beans and lay on top.

Mix the sour cream with the tomato salsa and layer it on the mashed beans.

Add a layer of the chopped roma tomatoes. Add a layer of the chopped scallions (save a little for a garnish).

Add a layer of the tasty grated cheese and for the final layer, add a sprinkling of parmesan shavings on top. Garnish with a few chopped scallions.

This dip is excellent with tortilla or corn chips. Or simply a side plate with fork.

Garlic-crusted Broad Bean Puree

Serves 4 / Preparation: 10 mins / Total cooking time: 25 mins

7 oz (200 g) fresh broad beans, peeled

1 bunch spring onions

1 tablespoon butter

1 head baby cos lettuce, shredded

4 slices white or sourdough bread

2 cloves garlic

1 teaspoon thyme, chopped
(can also use dried)

salt and black pepper, to taste

Preheat the oven to 400°F (200°C).

Cook the beans in boiling salted water until tender and drain.

Trim off green tops of spring onions and finely slice the bulbs. Heat the butter in a saucepan and lightly cook the onions and lettuce until translucent.

Combine onions, lettuce and beans in a food processor and pulse until you have a coarse puree. Season. Spread the puree into gratin dishes.

Cut the crusts from the bread and combine with the garlic and thyme in a food processor. Process until you have a fine crumb. Spread a layer over the bean puree and bake in the oven for 8 minutes until golden and crisp.

White Haricot Beans and Roasted Garlic Dip

Serves 6 / Preparation time: 10 mins / Cooking time: 40 mins

1 head of garlic
olive oil
3 sprigs thyme
1 x 14 oz (400 g) can haricot beans (lima
    beans can also be used), drained and

rinsed
2 tablespoons extra virgin olive oil
1½ tablespoons lemon juice
1 teaspoon sea salt flakes
ground black pepper

ROASTED GARLIC

Preheat oven to 350°F (180°C).

Trim top and quarter the whole garlic head to expose cloves. Blanch in boiling water for 5 minutes. Drain well. Discard any loose skin and puncture sides and top of the clove with a fork. Place into a ceramic dish and drizzle generously with oil then sprinkle with thyme, flaky salt and ground black pepper. Roast for 40 minutes, or until the cloves start to pop out of their skins. Cool and squeeze the garlic out. Store in a covered container. The garlic can be refrigerated for up to five days.

DIP

Place the haricot beans, 1 teaspoon roasted garlic, oil and lemon juice into a food processor fitted with a metal blade and process until smooth. Season with salt and pepper.

This dip can be refrigerated, covered, for up to 3–4 days or served immediately.

Serve on crusty bread or in a bowl with vegetables for dipping.

SOUPS

Ham Hock and Bean Soup

Serves 8–10 / Preparation: 20 mins / Total cooking time: 2–3 hours

7 oz (200 g) dried cannellini beans

2 tablespoons olive oil

2 bacon rashers, rind removed and chopped

4 large onions, chopped

3 carrots, chopped

2 zucchini (courgette), chopped

3 stalks celery, chopped

8 cloves garlic, roughly chopped

2 potatoes, chopped

4 sprigs thyme, leaves only

2 bay leaves

1 ham hock (about 28 oz/800 g)

¼ (about 14 oz/400 g) white cabbage, finely
  shredded

7 oz (200 g) Brussels sprouts, roughly
  chopped

pinch of salt and ¼ teaspoon black pepper,
  for seasoning

flat-leaf parsley, chopped for serving

Soak the cannellini beans in cold water for at least 8 hours or overnight.

Heat the oil in a stockpot and cook bacon for 3–4 minutes until crisp. Add the onion, carrot, zucchini and celery and cook, stirring, for about 6–8 minutes until soft. Add the garlic and cook for another 2–3 minutes until translucent. Add the potato, thyme, bay leaves, ham hock, cabbage, stock and sprouts.

Drain beans, rinse and add to the pot. Add enough water to cover all the ingredients and bring to the boil. Reduce heat to a simmer, topping up water if necessary. Cook for 3–4 hours until ham hock meat is tender and falling off the bone.

Remove hock from pot and allow to cool slightly. Strip off the meat, throw away the bone and skin, roughly chop the meat.

Add chopped ham back to the pot and bring to the boil and then simmer for a further 15 minutes or until the beans are mushy and the broth is thick and cloudy, adding more water if it is too thick for your liking.

Serve in large bowls and sprinkle with chopped parsley on top.

This soup is another one that is safe to freeze for up to 3 months. Freeze without the parsley.

Lamb Shank, White Bean and Vegetable Soup

 Serves 4 / Preparation: 10 mins / Total cooking time: 2 hours 15 minutes

1 tablespoon olive oil

4 medium-sized lamb shanks

1 large brown onion, finely chopped

2 cloves garlic, finely chopped

4 medium carrots, thinly sliced

4 stalks celery, thinly sliced

5 cups good-quality beef stock

4 cups water

1 x14 oz (400 g) can cannellini beans, drained
   and rinsed

salt and pepper to taste

flat-leaf parsley, chopped for garnish

crusty bread stick

Heat oil in large heavy-based saucepan and cook lamb shanks until well browned all over. Remove shanks from pan and set aside.

Add onion, garlic, carrot and celery to pan. Cook, stirring, until onion is just tender.

Add beef stock and water to pan and bring to the boil. Return lamb shanks to the pan and lower heat to medium–low. Simmer, partially covered for 2 hours, stirring occasionally, until shanks are tender. Add more water if required.

Add cannellini beans and cook until heated through, about 5 minutes. Season to taste with cracked black pepper and sea salt.

Serve garnished with chopped parsley and crusty bread.

Laksa Soup

Serves 4 / Preparation time: 10 mins / Cooking time: 10 mins

¼ cup laksa paste

3 cups chicken stock

3 cups cold water

1 x 14 fl oz (400 ml) can coconut milk

9 oz (250 g) rice vermicelli noodles, dried

9 oz (250 g) Hokkien noodles

14 oz (400 g) green king shrimp (prawns),

peeled, deveined but leave tails on

2 cups bean sprouts

½ cup fresh cilantro (coriander) leaves

1 long red chilli, thinly sliced

lime or lemon wedges, to serve

Heat laksa paste in a heavy-based saucepan over medium heat for about two minutes. Add stock, cold water and coconut milk. Cover and bring to the boil. Add noodles. Simmer for four minutes or until noodles are tender.

Add shrimp. Simmer for two to three minutes or until the shrimp turn pink.

Divide mixture between 4 bowls. Top with bean sprouts, coriander and chilli.

Serve with lime or lemon wedges on the side as some people like to add this refreshing lift and some do not.

You can also add deep-fried tofu puffs (found in Asian grocery stores).

Seafood and White Bean Soup

6 cups chicken stock

¼ teaspoon saffron threads

1 x 4 oz (4 oz/120 g) chorizo sausage, cut into
*   ½ in (5 mm) slices*

14 oz (400 g) green shrimp (prawn) meat,
*   head and tails removed*

1 x 14 oz (400 g) can crushed tomatoes

1 medium brown onion, roughly chopped

1 medium red bell pepper (capsicum),
*   seeded, cut into large chunks*

3 cloves garlic, peeled

2 tablespoons olive oil

2 teaspoons smoked paprika

1 cup (7 oz/200 g) arborio rice

14 oz (400 g) marinara mix

12 cleaned, de-bearded mussels

1 x 14 oz (400 g) can cannellini beans, rinsed
*   and drained*

½ cup flat-leaf parsley, chopped

olive oil and lemon wedges, to serve

French baguette, broken into chunks

Combine stock and saffron in a medium saucepan and bring to the boil. Reduce the heat to a low simmer.

Place a large saucepan over medium-high heat and cook chorizo for 2 minutes or until golden. Remove to bowl, leaving oil in the pan. Add shrimp to the pan, cooking until slightly golden and just cooked. Remove from the pan.

Place tomatoes, onion, bell pepper and garlic in food processor and puree until smooth. Add olive oil to the pan, then tomato mixture. Stir until most of the moisture has evaporated, about 10–15 minutes. The mixture will start to break up and become more paste-like when it is ready. Add paprika and stir for 1 minute, then add rice and stir to coat.

Pour in one-third of the stock mixture and stir to combine. Pour in remainder of the stock and bring to the boil, reduce to a simmer and cook on low heat, uncovered, for 15 minutes. Add marinara mix, mussels and cannellini beans, simmer for 10 minutes on low heat until mussels open up. Return shrimp and chorizo to pan, season to taste if needed.

Spoon into serving bowls, sprinkle over parsley, drizzle over with olive oil and serve with lemon wedges on the side. Cut baguette into large chunks to serve.

Carrot, Bean and Ginger Soup

Serves 4–6 / Preparation: 10 mins / Cooking time: 40 mins

6 large carrots, roughly chopped
½ teaspoon fennel seeds
3 tablespoons olive oil
1 onion, roughly chopped
3 cloves garlic, thinly sliced
2 stalks celery, chopped

1.5 in (3 cm) piece ginger, grated
3 thyme sprigs, leaves removed
6 cups vegetable stock
1 cup butter beans, washed and drained
salt and black pepper, to season

Preheat the oven to 350°F (180°C). Line a baking tray with baking paper. Place carrot, fennel seeds and 2 tablespoons oil in a bowl, season and toss. Tip onto tray, distribute evenly and roast for 30 minutes until tender.

Heat the remaining tablespoon of oil in a large saucepan over medium heat. Add the onion and garlic, then cook for about 3 minutes until softened. Add the celery and cook for a further 3 minutes until softened. Add the ginger, thyme, stock and roasted carrot, then cook, stirring occasionally for 25–30 minutes until liquid is slightly reduced. Transfer to a blender and whiz until smooth.

Return soup to the saucepan and add the white and butter beans and heat until warmed through.

Serve in bowls with an extra sprig of thyme for decoration.

White Bean Soup with Kransky

Serves 6 / Preparation: 10 mins / Total cooking time: 30 mins

1 tablespoon extra virgin olive oil

5 oz (150 g) bacon, chopped into small pieces

2 medium carrots, sliced

2 small leeks, sliced in 1 in (2 cm) pieces

53 fl oz (1.5 L) chicken stock

1 x 14 oz (400 g) can cannellini beans, rinsed
    and drained

2 bay leaves

10½ oz (300 g) kransky, sliced

1 large cabbage leaf, shredded

salt and pepper, to taste

pinch of nutmeg

chopped parsley, to garnish

Heat oil in pan and gently cook bacon, carrots and leeks for 5 minutes. Add chicken stock, cannellini beans, bay leaves and kransky slices and simmer for 20 minutes.

Add cabbage and simmer for a further 5 minutes. Season with salt and pepper and nutmeg. Ladle into serving bowls and sprinkle with chopped parsley.

Barley, Bean and Vegetable Soup with Crunch!

Serves 6 / Preparation: 10 mins / Total cooking time: 35 mins

2 tablespoons virgin olive oil

1 large red onion, chopped

1 medium parsnip, chopped

2 stalks celery, chopped

4 cloves garlic, chopped

1 cup tomato puree (passata)

4 cups vegetable stock

4 cups water

2 medium red bell peppers (capsicums), chopped

1 x 14 oz (400 g) can cannellini beans, drained

½ cup pearl barley

¼ cup fresh basil, loosely torn

CRUNCH ELEMENT

2 tablespoons pumpkin seeds

2 tablespoons sunflower seeds

2 tablespoons pine nuts

½ cup parmesan cheese, grated

Heat 1 tablespoon of the oil in a large saucepan over medium heat. Cook onion, parsnip, celery and garlic for approximately 5 minutes, stirring constantly until onion is softened.

Add tomato puree, stock and water and bring to the boil. Stir in the bell pepper, beans and barley. Simmer, covered, for 25 minutes until the barley is tender.

To make the crunch element, heat the remaining oil in a small frying pan over medium to high heat. Cook seeds and pine nuts, stirring until browned lightly. Remove from the pan quickly, so they don't continue to cook and burn.

Just before serving, stir the basil into the soup. Ladle the soup into bowls, sprinkle the crunch element on top and then top with parmesan.

This is a hearty soup with lots of surprises for your mouth.

Chunky Tuscan Bean Soup

Serves 4 / Preparation: 20 mins / Total cooking time: 20 mins

1 tablespoon olive oil

¾ oz (25 g) unsalted butter

1 large onion, roughly chopped

2 stalks celery, de-stringed and roughly
   chopped

1 large carrot, roughly chopped

2 cloves garlic, crushed

3 thyme sprigs, leaves removed

2 rosemary sprigs, leaves removed and

roughly chopped

1 x 14 oz (400 g) can chopped tomatoes

4 cups vegetable stock

1 x 14 oz (400 g) can cannellini beans, rinsed
   and drained

¼ (about 14 oz/400 g) Savoy cabbage, thinly
   sliced

rock salt and black pepper, for seasoning

In a large saucepan, heat the oil and butter over a medium heat. Add the onion and celery and cook for about 5 minutes or until starting to soften.

Add the carrot, garlic and herbs and cook, stirring occasionally, for 5–10 minutes until the carrot starts to soften.

Add the tomatoes and stock and bring to a simmer. Add the cannellini beans and thinly sliced cabbage. Season to taste. Simmer for a further 15 minutes or until tender.

This is a tasty soup served with chunky bread. For something different, place a good teaspoon or two of pesto on top. You could also garnish with parmesan flakes.

Mexican Bean Soup

Serves 4 / Preparation time: 20 mins / Cooking time: 30 mins

2 tablespoons olive oil

1 medium red bell pepper (capsicum), chopped

1 medium green bell pepper (capsicum), chopped

2 cloves garlic, crushed

2 cups vegetable stock

1 x 14 oz (400 g) can diced tomatoes

¼ cup semi-sundried tomatoes, drained and chopped

2 tablespoons tomato paste

2 teaspoons ground cumin

½ teaspoon chilli powder

1 teaspoon dried oregano

½ teaspoon salt

2½ fl oz (80 ml) water

1 x 14 oz (400 g) can red kidney beans, drained and rinsed

½ red onion, sliced

½ bunch cilantro (coriander) leaves

7 oz (200 g) crumbled feta

warmed tortillas, to serve

Reserve 1 tablespoon red and green bell peppers to serve.

Heat oil in a saucepan over medium heat and cook peppers and garlic for 4 minutes or until softened. Stir in stock, tomatoes, chopped sun-dried tomatoes, tomato paste, spices and the water.

Bring to the boil and simmer, stirring occasionally, for 20 minutes. Add the drained beans and simmer for a further 5 minutes until all flavours are blended.

Place hot soup in bowls and top with reserved bell pepper, red onion, coriander leaves and feta.

Serve with warm tortillas.

White Bean and Artichoke Soup

Serves 8 / Preparation: 20 mins / Cooking time: 35 mins

4 oz (125 g) butter

2 medium brown onions, sliced

2 leeks, trimmed and sliced

2 stalks celery, trimmed and sliced

1 x 14 oz (400 g) can cannellini beans,
    drained and rinsed

1 medium potato, peeled and sliced

2 lb (1 kg) Jerusalem artichokes, peeled and
    sliced

2 cloves garlic, peeled and sliced

52 fl oz (1.5 L) chicken stock (can use
    vegetable)

3½ fl oz (100 ml) cream

salt and freshly ground black pepper to taste

plain Greek yoghurt, to serve

In a heavy-based saucepan, place butter and cook the onions, leeks, celery and potatoes until softened. Add the artichoke, garlic and chicken stock. Cook until the artichokes are tender.

Strain the soup, reserving all the liquid. Place the cooked vegetables and the white beans with about 7 fl oz (200 ml) of the soup liquid in a blender and blend until smooth. Add the cream and continue to blend.

Return soup to the saucepan and bring to a simmer. Before serving, adjust seasonings. Place in a bowl to serve and add a dollop of yoghurt

SALADS

Black Turtle Beans and Ham Salad

Serves 8 / Preparation: 20 mins
Total cooking time: 45 mins and/or traditional method of soaking 6–8 hours or overnight

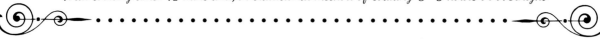

13 oz (375 g) black turtle beans

9 oz (250 g) ham, diced

2 vine-ripened tomatoes, diced

½ cup chopped scallions (shallots)

1 medium carrot, diced or shredded

sea salt and black pepper, to taste

¼ cup shaved parmesan cheese

1 tablespoon chopped fresh parsley

¼ cup store-bought Greek salad dressing

Rinse the beans thoroughly then place in a saucepan and cover with water. There should be about 3 cups of water for every cup of beans.

Bring to the boil and simmer for approximately 45 minutes until tender, skimming if necessary. Drain and cool.

Place the beans and ingredients in a bowl and toss well in the Greek salad dressing, cover and refrigerate for approximately 1 hour.

To serve, mix well and scatter with parmesan cheese and chopped parsley.

Green Bean, Craisin and Caper Salad

Serves 6–8 / Preparation: 15 mins / Total cooking time: 5 mins

1 lb (500 g) green beans, trimmed and halved
  on the diagonal
1 lemon, rind removed with potato peeler and
  thinly sliced
2 tablespoons craisins (dried cranberries)

2 tablespoons verjuice
2 fl oz (60ml) olive oil
1 tablespoon salted capers, rinsed
sea salt and black pepper

Blanch beans in boiling salted water in a saucepan with lemon rind for 2–3 minutes or until tender. Drain and refresh beans and lemon rind in iced water. Drain and set aside.

Combine craisins and verjuice in a small bowl and microwave on low setting for 20 seconds to plump up.

Heat olive oil in a small frying pan over medium heat. Add capers and fry for 1–2 minutes, add reserved lemon rind and the craisin and verjuice mixture. Cook until heated through.

Toss caper mixture through beans and transfer to serving platter. Season with sea salt and ground black pepper.

Green Beans and Pineapple Salad

 Serves 6 / Preparation: 10 mins / Total cooking time: 5 mins

36 oz (1 kg) green beans, top and tailed

2 tablespoons virgin olive oil

1 tablespoon raspberry vinegar

1 tablespoon chopped walnuts

1 tablespoon thinly sliced sweetened dried pineapple (fresh can be substituted)

Wash and trim the green beans. Place in a saucepan and cover with water. Bring to the boil and then turn the heat down and simmer until the beans are tender but still bright green, about 5 minutes. Rinse in cold water to bring out colour.

Whisk the olive oil and raspberry vinegar in a large bowl, add cooked beans and toss to coat.

Plate beans and sprinkle over walnuts and pineapple.

If you prefer, you can substitute the walnuts for coconut chips.

Kidney Bean, Red Onion and Mixed Cherry Tomato Salad

½ red onion, thinly sliced

2 tablespoons red wine vinegar

9 oz (250 g) sweet cherry tomatoes

1 teaspoon sea salt, preferably fine

2 x 14 oz (400 g) cans red kidney beans, drained and rinsed

2 tablespoons extra virgin olive oil

2 tablespoons cilantro (coriander) leaves

Place the onion and vinegar in a small bowl. Cover and set aside to macerate for up to 3 hours at room temperature.

To prepare the salad, halve the tomatoes and place in the serving bowl.

Sprinkle with 1 teaspoon of sea salt.

Add the prepared kidney beans, onion mixture, cilantro and olive oil.

Toss gently to mix before serving.

You could substitute roma tomatoes as they also have a strong flavour if you aren't into sweet tomatoes.

Pancetta, Baby Bean and Egg Salad

Serves 4 / Preparation: 20 mins / Total cooking time: 10 mins

20 baby Roma tomatoes

4 fl oz (125 ml) virgin olive oil, plus extra to drizzle

8 slices pancetta

3 anchovy fillets

2 teaspoons Dijon mustard

2 tablespoons red wine vinegar

5 free-range eggs

10 ½ oz (300 g) baby green beans

2 baby cos lettuce, inside leaves only

flat-leaf parsley, chopped, for garnish

Preheat the oven to 350°F (180°C). Place the tomatoes on a baking tray covered with baking paper and drizzle with olive oil. Place pancetta on a separate paper-lined tray. Put both trays in oven and roast for 5 minutes or until tomatoes start to split and the pancetta is crispy (tomatoes may need longer than pancetta in oven).

Remove from the oven and cool tomatoes for 5 minutes, then gently cut in half. Drain pancetta on a paper towel and, when cool, break into pieces.

Blend anchovy, mustard, vinegar and 1 egg in a food processor, until just combined. With the motor running, slowly add the oil through the feed tube until the dressing has thickened. Set aside.

Place remaining eggs in medium saucepan with cold water. Bring to the boil, then cook for 3 minutes until soft-boiled (cook for a few extra minutes if you prefer your eggs hard-boiled). Remove from heat, drain and refresh under cold water. Carefully peel eggs, cut in half and set aside. Blanch beans in boiling salted water for 2–3 minutes until just tender. Drain and refresh in cold water.

Divide lettuce, beans and tomato amongst 4 bowls and top with eggs and pancetta. Drizzle with dressing and sprinkle parsley on top.

Roast Beetroot, Bean and Feta Salad

 Serves 8 / Preparation: 20 mins / Total cooking time: 30 mins

6–8 medium-sized beetroot, scrubbed,
    peeled and cut into quarters
2 tablespoons extra virgin olive oil
7 oz (200 g) green beans, trimmed
2 oz (50 g) yellow beans, trimmed
8 oz (220 g) feta, crumbled

½ cup fresh walnuts

DRESSING
¼ cup walnut oil
¼ cup extra virgin olive oil
2 tablespoons lemon juice

Preheat the oven to 375°F (190°C).

Toss the beetroot in olive oil and place in a lined baking tray. Bake in the oven for 25–30 minutes, turning gently, until the beetroot is tender. Set aside.

Cook beans for 3–4 minutes in boiling water. Rinse and refresh in cold water.

Place on serving platter and top with the warmed beetroot, feta and walnuts.

Mix the dressing ingredients together. Drizzle over beetroot and beans. Serve immediately.

Thai Beef and Snake Bean Salad

 Serves 4 / Preparation: 15 mins / Total cooking time: 10 mins

8 snake beans, cut into 1.5 in (3 cm) lengths

1 lb (500 g) fillet steak

salt and pepper

olive oil, for frying

juice of 2 limes

zest of 1 lime

2 tablespoons fish sauce

1 tablespoon tamari sauce

6 scallions (shallots), sliced thinly on an angle

1 Lebanese cucumber, seeded and sliced on an angle

2 long red chillies, deseeded and thinly sliced

½ cup Thai basil leaves

½ cup cilantro (coriander) leaves

handful of mixed lettuce

1 cup bean shoots

Blanch snake beans in boiling salted water for 4 minutes. Drain and refresh in cold water.

Season steak with salt and pepper. Heat olive oil in a medium-sized frying pan on medium to high heat. Add steak and cook for 2–3 minutes each side for medium rare, or to your liking. Remove steak from pan and rest, uncovered, for 5 minutes.

Meanwhile, mix the lime juice and zest with fish and tamari sauces in a large bowl. Add remaining ingredients and toss to combine. Slice the fillet steak thinly and toss with salad and serve while still warm.

MAINS

Borlotti Bean Meatloaf

Serves 4 / Preparation: 15 mins
Total cooking time: 20 mins after preparation of beans

6 ½ oz (190 g) dried borlotti beans

1½ cups water

3 tablespoons cranberry jam

2 tablespoons lemon juice

½ teaspoon black pepper

1 lb (500 g) lean ground beef

1 small onion, grated

¼ cup dry breadcrumbs

1 egg, beaten

¼ teaspoon cinnamon

salt and pepper

2 tablespoons olive oil

1 large onion, sliced

cranberry jam, to serve

Prepare the beans by soaking them for 6–8 hours. Drain the beans then place them in fresh water and boil them for about 30 minutes. Alternatively, you can boil the beans for 55 minutes or until tender.

Preheat the oven to 350°F (180°C).

In a separate saucepan, heat the water, jam, lemon juice and black pepper over a low heat until it starts to bubble. Remove from the heat and allow to cool slightly.

Place ground beef in a large bowl with the grated onion, breadcrumbs, egg and cinnamon with a pinch of salt and pepper.

Heat the olive oil in a saucepan and fry the sliced onion over a low heat, until transparent. Add drained tender beans to pan and stir. Add to meat mixture along with the cranberry sauce, reserving a ¼ cup of sauce to coat the top of the meatloaf.

Place mixture in a lined loaf tin and bake for 35 minutes. Once cooked, remove the meatloaf from the tin and glaze the top with the reserved sauce. Or, if you prefer, place the sauce in a jug to accompany the meatloaf when serving.

Serve with a green salad, crusty bread and some cranberry jam.

Greek Lamb Cutlets and White Beans

Serves: 4 / Preparation: 15 mins / Total cooking time: 25 mins

1 tablespoon olive oil

1 medium brown onion, finely chopped

2 cloves garlic, crushed

*2 x 14 oz (400 g) cans cannellini beans,
    rinsed and drained*

3 large ripe tomatoes, chopped

salt and cracked black pepper

olive oil spray

12 lamb cutlets, trimmed of fat

1 tablespoon dried oregano

1 tablespoon flat-leaf parsley, chopped

Heat oil in saucepan over medium heat. Add onion and garlic and cook for 5 minutes or until onion is soft. Add cannellini beans, tomatoes and a little water; season with salt and black pepper. Bring to the boil, cover and simmer on low heat for about 10 minutes to allow the sauce to thicken. Remove from the heat.

Preheat a chargrill or barbecue on high heat. Spray lamb cutlets with olive oil and rub in oregano, pepper and salt. Cook the lamb for 3–4 minutes each side for pink (cooking time will differ on size of the cutlets) or a little longer for medium to well done.

Add parsley to bean mixture and transfer to serving plates. Top with cutlets.

Braised Meatballs
with Cannellini Beans

Serves 4–6 / Preparation: 30 mins / Total cooking time: 35 mins

1 lb (500 g) pork and veal ground (mince)

½ cup fresh white breadcrumbs

1 onion, finely chopped

1 egg, lightly beaten

2 teaspoons chopped fresh rosemary

1 tablespoon olive oil

1 lb (250 g) rindless bacon, coarsely chopped

2 cloves garlic, crushed

1 lb 9 oz (700 ml) jar tomato puree (passata)

1 x 14 oz (400 g) can cannellini beans, rinsed and drained

6 potatoes for mashing, peeled and cut into chunks

1 tablespoon butter

½ cup milk

flat-leaf parsley for serving, chopped

Combine mince, breadcrumbs, onion, egg and rosemary and mix well in large bowl. Roll tablespoons of mixture into rough balls.

Heat oil on high heat in large frying pan. Cook meatballs for 5 minutes, shaking pan to brown all over. Remove and set aside.

Add bacon to same pan. Cook for 5 minutes or until golden in colour. Stir in garlic and cook for 30 seconds. Reduce heat to medium. Mix in passata and bring to a simmer.

Arrange meatballs in sauce. Simmer, covered, 12–15 minutes, until cooked through. Add cannellini beans and heat through for a few minutes.

Cook potatoes in salted water until soft. Drain and mash, add butter and milk to taste.

Pile mashed potato on plates, top with meatball mixture and sprinkle with chopped parsley.

Chilli Con Carne

Serves 4

1 tablespoon light olive oil

1 onion, chopped

1 clove garlic, chopped

1 green bell pepper (capsicum),
  roughly chopped

1 lb (500 g) ground (minced) beef

4 fl oz (125 ml) cup water

1 tablespoon tomato paste

1 teaspoon chilli powder

¼ teaspoon cumin

1 teaspoon soft brown sugar

½ teaspoon salt

pinch of cayenne pepper

1 teaspoon chopped fresh basil (dry is also
  good)

1 x 14 oz (400 g) can crushed tomatoes

1 tablespoon cider or red wine

1 x 14 oz (400 g) can red kidney beans,
  rinsed and drained

salt and ground black pepper, to taste

jalapenos, chopped, to taste

Preheat the oven to 400°F (200°C).

Heat oil in a large heavy-based pan and add the onion, garlic and bell pepper. Stir over a medium heat for 5 minutes, until soft. Add the beef and cook over high heat for 5 minutes until well browned.

Mix in the water, tomato puree, chilli powder, cumin, brown sugar, salt, cayenne pepper and basil to the pan. Cook for a further 2 minutes. Add the crushed tomatoes and stir to combine.

Simmer for 30 minutes, stirring occasionally. Add the cider or red wine, the kidney beans and season if needed. Heat through for 5 minutes.

You can also add some chopped jalapenos if you like it a little hotter to taste.

Pulled Lamb with Butter Beans

1 tablespoon olive oil

sea salt, to taste

zest and juice of 1 lemon

2 teaspoons ground cumin

3 teaspoons ground coriander

½ teaspoon chilli flakes

1 lamb shoulder, bone in, trimmed with
    shank attached

2 medium carrots, thickly sliced

10 eschallots, peeled

8 cloves garlic, peeled

70 fl oz (2 L) good-quality vegetable stock

2 x 14 oz (400 g) cans butter beans, drained
    and rinsed

3 teaspoons balsamic vinegar

½ cup flat-leaf parsley, chopped

½ fresh cilantro (coriander), chopped

3 teaspoons lemon juice

seasonal green vegetables, steamed

crusty French stick, to serve

Combine olive oil, sea salt, lemon juice and zest, cumin, coriander and chilli flakes in a bowl. Rub mixture over the lamb shoulder. Put marinated lamb in a sealed bag and refrigerate overnight to absorb the flavours.

Remove lamb from the fridge 1 hour before cooking.

Preheat the oven to 350°F (180°C).

Place lamb in a baking dish with the carrots, eschallots, garlic and vegetable stock.

Cook lamb, uncovered, for 30 minutes, then baste with stock. Reduce the oven temperature to 285°F (140°C) and cook for 3 hours, uncovered, basting occasionally.

Cover the lamb loosely with foil and cook for 2 hours. During the last hour of cooking, add the butter beans to the pan (adding too early can make the beans mushy) . The lamb is ready when it almost falls off the bone.

Remove lamb from the oven and let it rest, covered loosely with foil.

Gently remove the butter beans from the pan with a slotted spoon and set aside.

Put the pan juices, vegetables and balsamic vinegar into a blender and blend roughly. Transfer to a small saucepan and heat over a low heat to warm through (do not boil). Gently fold through the reserved butter beans. Add chopped parsley, coriander and lemon juice.

Transfer lamb to serving platter and serve with butter bean sauce and seasonal green vegetables. Soak up sauce with a crusty French baguette torn into chunky slices.

Borlotti Bean Barbecue Hot Dog

Serves 4 / Preparation: 10 mins / Total cooking time: 15 mins

3 tablespoons coconut oil
1 large onion, finely chopped
2 cloves garlic, finely chopped
1 x 14 oz (400 g) can borlotti beans, rinsed
    and drained

2 tablespoons seeded or mild English
    mustard
1 cup grated cheddar cheese

Heat 1 tablespoon of coconut oil in a medium-sized saucepan. Gently fry onion and garlic for 3–5 minutes until soft and translucent.

Add beans to onion and garlic. Using a potato masher, mash with 2 tablespoons oil. Cook for 10 minutes, stirring to prevent sticking, until the beans have absorbed the oil. If still sticking, add a little more oil.

Shape into a thick sausage, then transfer to a plate with a spatula, run the mustard down the middle of the sausage and top with cheese.

This bean sausage is best served immediately while hot.

Italian Sausage Bean Hot Pot

Serves 4–6 / Preparation: 20 mins / Total cooking time: 60 mins

2 tablespoons olive oil
28 oz (800 g) Italian sausages
4 onions, thinly sliced
1 cup beef stock
2 cups tomato puree (passata)
15 fl oz (440 ml) can Guinness or any stout
   beer

⅓ cup brown sugar
2 bay leaves
2 x 14 oz (400 g) cans borlotti beans, rinsed
   and drained
chopped parsley, to garnish

Preheat the oven to 350°F (180°C).

Heat the oil in a large flameproof casserole or heavy-based saucepan over medium heat. Cook sausages for 5–6 minutes until browned. Set aside. Cool and cut into 1 in (2.5 cm) pieces. Drain some of the oil from the pan if necessary. Add the onion to the pan and cook for 5–6 minutes until soft. Add stock, tomato puree, beer, sugar and bay leaves, then bring to the boil.

Reduce heat to medium–low and return sausages to the casserole or pan with beans. Transfer to the oven for 40 minutes or slowly cook on top of stove until sauce thickens.

To serve, stir in chopped parsley. An ideal accompaniment for this is mashed potatoes.

Butter Bean Boats

Serves 4 / Preparation time: 25 mins
/ Total cooking time: 1 hour 45 mins

1 tablespoon olive oil, plus extra to rub and drizzle

2 butternut pumpkin, halved lengthways, seeds scooped out

1 x 14 oz (400 g) can butter beans, drained and rinsed

1 egg, beaten

1½ oz (40 g) butter

1 small onion, finely chopped

2 cloves garlic, crushed

½ teaspoon fresh rosemary leaves, finely chopped plus extra sprigs to decorate

3½ oz (100 g) mushrooms, thinly sliced

½ teaspoon salt

½ teaspoon cracked black pepper

Preheat the oven to 350°F (180°C).

Rub olive oil into pumpkin halves and place on a tray lined with baking paper. Cover with foil and roast for 1 hour. Remove foil and return to oven for a further 15 minutes or until tender and roasted. Cool slightly.

Place butter beans in a bowl and mash. Mix in egg and add salt and pepper.

Place 1 tablespoon oil and half the butter in a pan over a medium heat. Cook onion and garlic for 2–3 minutes until soft and slightly brown. Add the rest of the butter to pan, along with the chopped rosemary and sliced mushrooms and cook for 2 minutes. Transfer to a bowl and mix with the butter bean mixture.

Fill the cavity in the butternut pumpkins with the bean mixture while the pumpkin is still on the baking tray and place back in the oven for 5 minutes.

To serve, place on a serving platter and decorate with rosemary sprigs.

This is a meal that can be eaten by vegetarians, accompanied by salad or steamed green vegetables, or as a side dish with any meat or fish.

Layered Tortilla Chilli Con Carne

Serves 4 / Preparation: 40 mins / Total cooking time: 20 mins

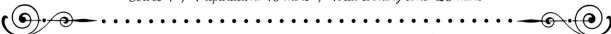

8 mini flour tortillas

1 tablespoon olive oil

1 large onion, finely chopped

2 cloves garlic, crushed

1 lb 9 oz (700 g) premium ground (minced)
   beef

1 oz (30 g) packet mild taco mix

1 x 14 oz (400 g) can chopped tomatoes

1 teaspoon crushed chillies [AQ: Dried chilli
   flakes?]

2 x 14 oz (410 g) cans red kidney beans,
   drained

pepper and salt, to taste

olive oil spray

2 cups grated tasty cheese

13 oz (375 g) jar tomato salsa

Greek yoghurt, to serve

mixed salad leaves, to serve

Preheat the oven to 350°F (180°C).

Place tortillas in a single layer on two large oven trays. Bake in the oven for 8 minutes or until golden in colour. Set aside.

Meanwhile, heat the olive oil in a frying pan and add onion and garlic. Cook, stirring occasionally, until soft. Add mince and taco mix. Cook for 3–4 minutes, breaking up lumps. Add tomatoes, crushed chilli and beans. Season with salt and pepper. Cook, stirring occasionally, for 7 minutes or until mixture thickens slightly. Cool.

Line two baking dishes with foil and spray with oil. Place 2 tortillas in the base of each pan. Spread generous cup of beef mixture over the top of each. Sprinkle each with about ¼ cup cheese and top with another tortilla. Repeat second layer, finishing with cheese. Top with tomato salsa.

Bake in the oven for 20 minutes or until heated through.

Remove baking dishes from the oven and slide the layered tortillas onto four serving plates. Dollop with Greek yoghurt. Serve with mixed salad leaves.

Jalapeno chillies can be added as a side dish for additional flavour.

Lemon Garlic Chicken with Salsa Verde and Two-bean Salad

Serves 4 / Preparation: 10 mins / Total cooking time: 10 mins

juice and zest of 1 lemon

1 tablespoon virgin olive oil

2 cloves garlic, crushed

36 oz (1 kg) chicken thigh fillets

1 x 14 oz (400 g) can borlotti beans, drained
and rinsed

1 x 14 oz (400 g) can cannellini beans,
drained and rinsed

5 oz (150 g) baby spinach leaves

5 oz (150 g) grape tomatoes, halved

2 tablespoons virgin olive oil

SALSA VERDE

1 cup mint leaves

1 cup flat-leaf parsley

2 tablespoons capers

1 clove garlic, finely chopped

¼ cup virgin olive oil

juice of 1 lemon

Combine the lemon juice and zest, olive oil and garlic in a large bowl. Season generously with salt and pepper. Cut chicken fillets in half, then slice in half horizontally so the pieces are thinner. Put the sliced chicken pieces in the lemon and garlic mixture and leave to marinade for 5 minutes.

In a large frying pan over high heat cook the chicken for 4–5 minutes each side or until cooked through. Set aside and cover with foil to keep warm.

To make the salsa verde, combine mint, parsley, capers and garlic in a food processor and pulse until chopped. Add olive oil and lemon juice and pulse until all ingredients are combined.

Combine borlotti and cannellini beans, spinach leaves, tomatoes and extra virgin olive oil in a bowl and mix gently. Transfer to a serving platter, top with chicken and serve with the salsa verde.

Pork Shoulder with Spinach and Cannellini Beans

Serves 4 / Preparation: 10 mins / Total cooking time: 2½ hours

3 lb 8 oz (1.6 kg) pork shoulder
ground black pepper
¼ cup extra virgin olive oil
1 large onion, finely chopped
4 cloves garlic, crushed
1 large stalk celery with leaves, chopped
1 cup (250 ml) dry white wine
13 fl oz (375 ml) tomato puree (passata)

1 x 14 oz (400 g) can cannellini beans,
    drained and rinsed
4 tablespoons fresh sage leaves
7 oz (200 g) baby spinach leaves
2 tablespoons extra virgin olive oil
ground black pepper and sea salt, to taste
12 baby chat potatoes

Preheat the oven to 300°F (150°C).

Season the pork with pepper. Heat oil in a heavy-based ovenproof casserole dish over a medium–high heat and brown pork all over. Arrange onion, garlic and celery around the pork and sauté for 3 minutes. Add white wine, tomato puree and cannellini beans, cover and bring to the simmer. Bake, covered, for 2 hours until pork is soft. Remove pork from dish, cover with foil and set aside.

Cook chat potatoes in boiling salted water until tender.

Meanwhile, add sage leaves to pan juices and boil down until reduced by half. Season to taste and mix through spinach leaves, stirring until wilted. Stir in olive oil. Carve pork and serve with sauce and chat potatoes.

Pork Steaks with Black Bean and Avocado Salad

1 tablespoon red wine vinegar

2 teaspoons ground cumin

½ teaspoon chilli powder

sea salt and ground black pepper

4 x 5½ oz (160 g) lean pork medallion steaks

BLACK BEAN AND AVOCADO SALAD

1 x 14 oz (400 g) can black beans (or red
  kidney beans), drained and rinsed

1 large avocado, chopped

1 small carrot, shredded

1 large vine-ripened tomato, seeds removed,
  chopped

large pinch chilli powder

1 lime, skin removed, including white pith,
  flesh chopped

½ cup cilantro (coriander) leaves

1 tablespoon coconut oil

1 tablespoon red wine vinegar

Combine vinegar, cumin, chilli powder, salt and pepper in a bowl. Add pork and toss to thoroughly coat.

Heat large, lightly oiled frying pan over a medium to high heat. Add the pork medallions and cook for about 3–4 minutes on each side (for a medium steak).

Remove the pan from the heat and rest the pork, covered, for 5 minutes.

Gently toss all the salad ingredients in a large bowl. Serve the pork steaks with the bean salad. It's a fantastic flavour combination.

Rack of Lamb on Bean Puree

Serves 4 / Preparation: 20 mins / Total cooking time: 25 mins

4 x 4-point lamb racks

salt and black pepper

olive oil

7 oz (200 g) fresh broad beans, peeled

1 bunch scallions (spring onions)

1 tablespoon butter

1 clove garlic, finely diced

1 head baby cos lettuce, shredded

Preheat the oven to 400°F (200°F).

Season the lamb racks with salt and pepper, pressing it well into the flesh. Heat a frying pan with a little oil and seal the racks on all sides.

Place in an ovenproof dish and roast for approximately 8 minutes.

Remove from the oven and rest for another 8 minutes before serving.

While the meat is roasting, cook the beans in boiling salted water until tender. Drain and peel off the hard shell.

Finely slice the scallions. Heat the butter in a saucepan and lightly cook the scallions, garlic and lettuce until translucent.

Combine onions, garlic, lettuce and beans in a food processor and pulse until you have a coarse puree. Season to taste with salt and black pepper.

Warm plates in the oven as the puree cools. Pile the bean puree in the middle of the dish and place lamb rack on top. Serve this with some baby carrots, sweet corn and scalloped poatatoes and you have a fabulous dinner, full of wonderful spring flavours.

Thai Chicken Stir-Fry with Bean Sprouts

Serves 4 / Preparation: 20 mins / Total cooking ime: 15 mins

7 oz (200 g) dried rice stick noodles

1 teaspoon olive oil

10½ oz (300 g) chicken tenderloins, thinly sliced

7 oz (200 g) green beans, sliced on the diagonal

2 cloves garlic, crushed

1.5 in (3 cm) piece fresh ginger, peeled and grated

3 tablespoons sweet chilli sauce

2 tablespoons water

1 lb (500 g) baby buk choy, halved lengthways

2 tablespoons fish sauce

4 tablespoons lime juice plus an extra lime cut into wedges for serving

6 scallions (shallots), thinly sliced

2 cups bean sprouts

1 cup fresh cilantro (coriander), chopped

1 cup fresh mint leaves, chopped

2 small fresh red thai chillies, thinly sliced

Place noodles in a large heatproof bowl, cover with boiling water and stand until just tender. Drain and set aside.

Meanwhile, heat oil in a wok or heavy-based frying pan over medium heat and stir-fry the chicken quickly until just cooked. Add green beans, garlic, ginger, sweet chilli sauce and water to the wok (or pan) and stir-fry until the beans are just tender. If sticking, add a little more water.

Add buk choy, fish sauce, lime juice, scallions, bean sprouts and half the chopped herbs to the wok and mix together until hot.

Spread the rice noodles on a serving platter and spoon over the chicken from the wok. Scatter remaining herbs and chilli and serve with lime wedges.

Thai Pork Patties with Quinoa

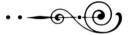

1 cup quinoa, rinsed

2 cups water

1 lb (500 g) ground (minced) pork

2 red chillies, finely chopped

1 tablespoon minced garlic

1 tablespoon lemongrass puree

2 eggs, beaten

3½ oz (100 g) green beans, finely sliced

3 scallions (spring onions), finely sliced

2 teaspoons coconut oil

mixed salad leaves, to dress platter

Place quinoa in a saucepan with two cups of water. Bring to the boil then simmer until all the water is absorbed. Take off heat and let cool.

Place in a large bowl, pork mince, chillies, garlic, lemongrass, beaten eggs, green beans, scallions and the cooled quinoa. Combine thoroughly using wet hands for easy handling and shape about 12 patties or 24 smaller balls ones for party fare.

Heat the coconut oil in a large non-stick frying pan over high heat. Add patties in batches. Reduce heat to medium and cook for about 3 minutes each side. If you want them brown, keep up the high heat but watch them carefully to make sure they don't burn.

When serving, add a green salad and any favourite dipping sauce.

Baked Salmon Fillets with Broad Beans

Serves 4 / Preparation: 10 mins / Total cooking time: 8 mins

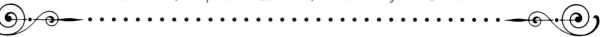

2 tablespoons flat-leaf parsley, finely
    chopped, plus extra for garnish
2½ fl oz (80 ml) good-quality olive oil
ground black pepper and sea salt
10½ oz (300 g) fresh or frozen peas
21 oz (600 g) podded fresh or frozen broad
    beans

4 x 7 oz (200 g) salmon fillets
2 lemons, cut into wedges
mixed green salad

Preheat the oven to 350°F (180°C). Warm an ovenproof baking dish in the oven before using. Combine chopped parsley and 2 fl oz (60 ml) of the olive oil in bowl, season with salt and pepper and set parsley oil aside.

Cook peas and broad beans in a saucepan of boiling water for 3 minutes or until tender, then drain. Peel and discard outer skin of broad beans when cooled down, then toss peas and beans in parsley oil and keep warm.

Coat salmon fillets with remaining olive oil and season with salt and pepper. Line the preheated baking dish with foil, place salmon in dish and bake for about 3–5 minutes or until cooked but still pink in the centre.

Remove from oven and serve salmon fillets with reserved warmed beans and parsley oil.

Calamari with White Bean Tabbouleh

Serves 4 / Preparation: 10 mins / Total cooking time: 5 mins

2 vine-ripened tomatoes
*1 x 14 oz (400 g) can cannellini beans, rinsed
  and drained*
2 tablespoons burghul (cracked wheat)
1 tablespoon extra virgin olive oil

*5 (about 10½ oz/300 g) cleaned calamari
  tubes, halved and scored*
1½ cups flat-leaf parsley, chopped
1 Lebanese cucumber, chopped finely
2 tablespoons lemon juice
lemon wedges, for serving

Chop tomatoes finely and place into a bowl with their own juice, beans and burghul. Mix together and set aside so the burghul soaks up the tomato juices.

Heat oil in a large non-stick frying pan over medium-high heat. Cook calamari in batches, stirring, for 2 minutes or until opaque and starting to turn golden. Remove from pan and slice into thick strips.

In a bowl combine beans and burghul mix, parsley, cucumber and lemon juice, toss to combine. Add the calamari and pan juices, season with sea salt and ground black pepper. Serve immediately with lemon wedges or separately as shown.

Linguine with Tuna, Borlotti Beans and Peas

Serves 4 / Preparation: 30 mins / Total cooking time: 45 mins

2 tablespoons oil

1 onion, finely chopped

4 cloves garlic, finely chopped

½ cup tomato paste

pinch of dried chilli flakes, to taste

5 ripe medium tomatoes, peeled, seeds
   removed and chopped

1 x 14 oz (400 g) can borlotti beans, rinsed
   and drained

1 x 14 oz (400 g) can tuna in spring water,
   drained

1 cup flat-leaf parsley, chopped

4 oz (120 g) frozen peas, thawed

14 oz (400 g) dried linguine pasta (or pasta of
   your choice)

Heat oil in a medium-sized saucepan over moderate heat. Add onion and cook for 2 minutes until soft. Add the chopped garlic and tomato paste and cook for 1 minute, stirring occasionally. Add the chilli flakes, tomato, drained borlotti beans and 1 cup water, then bring the sauce to a simmer.

Reduce heat to low and cook, stirring occasionally, for 15–20 minutes or until sauce has thickened. Stir in the tuna, parsley and peas, then cook for a further 2–3 minutes until the peas soften.

While sauce is simmering, cook linguine in a large pan of salted boiling water according to packet instructions. Drain.

Serve the pasta in individual bowls, pour over the sauce.

Serve with a bowl of parmesan cheese and a crusty loaf of Italian ciabatta bread and you have a quick and easy weeknight meal.

Shrimp with Cannellini Beans and Rocket Pesto

Serves 4 / Preparation: 10 mins / Total cooking time: 10 mins

2 tablespoons good-quality olive oil, plus extra to serve

3 cloves garlic, thinly sliced

2 zucchini (courgette), thinly sliced into rounds

¼ teaspoon chilli flakes, plus extra to serve if desired

2 x 14 oz (400 g) cans cannellini beans, rinsed and drained

3½ oz (100 ml) vegetable stock

24 green tiger shrimp (prawns), peeled and deveined with tails left on

Finely grated zest of 1 lemon

4 tablespoons flat-leaf parsley, chopped

ROCKET PESTO

3 anchovy fillets in oil, drained and finely chopped

1 clove garlic, crushed

1 bunch rocket leaves, (not stems) chopped

1 hard-boiled egg yolk, roughly chopped

¼ cup good-quality olive oil

Place all pesto ingredients in a blender and season with pepper. Blend until mixture is a thick puree. Add 1–2 tablespoons of water to loosen and pulse for a few seconds. Put pesto into a bowl, cover and refrigerate.

Heat 1 tablespoon of olive oil in a frying pan over a medium heat. Add garlic and cook for a few minutes until golden in colour. Add zucchini and chilli flakes and cook for 1 minute, stirring gently.

Add cannellini beans and vegetable stock and simmer for 5 minutes until warm. Mash one-quarter of the cooked beans roughly into the broth to thicken. Remove from heat and season to taste with pepper and salt.

Heat the remaining 1 tablespoon oil in separate frying pan over medium heat. Season shrimp and add to frying pan, cooking for 2–3 minutes until they have changed colour and are cooked through.

Remove pesto from fridge and fold into bean mixture. Spoon onto plates and top with shrimp, lemon zest, parsley, extra oil and chilli flakes.

Shrimp with Potato and Green Bean Salad

Serves 4 / Preparation: 15 mins / Total cooking time: 20 mins

 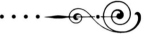

12 small kipfler potatoes, peeled and halved

1 tablespoon pistachio oil

1 tablespoon olive oil

2 tablespoons flat-leaf parsley, chopped

2 tablespoons fresh tarragon, chopped

2 tablespoons fresh chives, chopped

1 tablespoon olive oil, plus extra

2 scallions (spring onions), finely chopped

10½ oz (300 g) baby green beans, tails off

4 cups mixed salad leaves

2 tablespoons balsamic vinegar

2 tablespoons extra virgin olive oil

1 tablespoon extra virgin olive oil (for cooking shrimp)

20 green tiger shrimp (prawns), peeled, deveined, tails intact

2 lemons, cut into wedges

Cook potatoes for about 10 minutes or until tender. Remove to large bowl and toss with pistachio and olive oils, parsley, tarragon and chives.

Heat extra 1 tablespoon olive oil in frying pan over low heat and cook scallion for 2 minutes until soft. Remove from pan and add to bowl with potatoes.

Cook beans in boiling salted water for 4–5 minutes until just tender. Drain and refresh in cold water, add to bowl with potatoes.

Add mixed salad leaves, balsamic vinegar and extra virgin olive oil to bowl and mix gently.

Heat extra virgin olive oil in frying pan or barbecue over medium–high heat. Season shrimp and cook, turning, for 2–3 minutes until golden and cooked through.

To serve, scatter potato salad mix onto serving platter and top with shrimp. Arrange lemon wedges around platter.

Mussels with Black Beans

Serves 4 / Preparation: 15 mins / Total cooking time: 8 mins

1 teaspoon salted black beans*, rinsed

¼ teaspoon superfine (caster) sugar

2 tablespoons peanut oil

5 cloves garlic, crushed

1 tablespoon fresh ginger, grated

4 scallions (spring onions), white and green parts thinly sliced and kept separate, plus extra slices for garnish

70 oz (2 kg) mussels, scrubbed and debearded

2 tablespoons tamari sauce

3 tablespoons Chinese rice wine*

4 fl oz (120 ml) good-quality chicken stock

½ cup cilantro (coriander) leaves, chopped plus extra for garnish

crusty baguette stick

Mash black beans and sugar in a bowl together to form a paste.

Heat the oil in a wok over medium–high heat. Add garlic, ginger and black bean paste and stir-fry for 2 minutes or until fragrant.

Add white part of the scallions and stir-fry for about 10 seconds, then add mussels, tamari sauce, rice wine and stock. Cover wok tightly with lid and steam the mussels, shaking the pan occasionally for 4–5 minutes or until mussels open. Remove unopened mussels from wok and do not use.

Add cilantro and green part of scallions to wok and fold through.

Divide mussels into four serving bowls and garnish with cilantro and extra scallions.

Serve with a crusty French bread stick.

Salted black beans are available from Asian supermarkets. Dry sherry can replace Chinese rice wine.

Moors and Christians Spanish Beans and Rice

Serves 4 / Preparation: 15 mins / Total cooking time: 35 mins

¼ cup olive oil

2½ cups green bell peppers (capsicums), seeded and diced

2½ cups white onions, diced

4 garlic cloves, peeled and diced

1 x 15 oz (440 g) black beans, drained and rinsed

1 teaspoon oregano

2 tablespoons tomato paste

3 teaspoons ground cumin

1 bay leaf

2 tablespoon white vinegar

36 fl oz (1 L) chicken or vegetable stock

3 cups long grain white rice, rinsed

2 teaspoons salt

½ teaspoon ground black pepper

Heat the olive oil in a large stockpot over a medium–high heat. Heat the onions and green peppers and stir until tender. Add diced garlic and cook for about 1 minute. Add the black beans, oregano, tomato paste, cumin, bay leaf and vinegar. Cook on a low heat for approximately 6 minutes, stirring gently.

Add the stock and rinsed rice. Bring to the boil, reduce heat to low, cover and cook about 25 minutes until the rice is fully and cooked.

Add salt and pepper, remove the bay leaf and serve.

Bean Marinara

1 tablespoon coconut oil
1 large red onion, thinly sliced
2 cloves garlic, chopped
1 x 14 oz (400 g) can crushed tomatoes
2 tablespoons tomato paste
1 x 1 lb (500 g) tomato passata
¼ teaspoon Italian dried mixed herbs
3½ oz (100 g) green beans

1 x 14 oz (420 g) can butter beans, drained
  and rinsed
1lb (500 g) seafood marinara mix
3½ oz (100 g) raw green shrimp (prawns)
1 tablespoon parsley, chopped
lemon wedges, to serve

In a large frying, pan heat oil and sauté onion and garlic until soft. Add crushed tomato, tomato paste, passatta and herbs. Simmer for 15 minutes.

Wash, top and tail green beans and cut into 1 in (2.5 cm) pieces. Add butter beans and green beans to sauce. Heat through. Add seafood mixture and extra prawns, cook until prawns turn red, about 2-3 minutes.

Serve while hot and add chopped parsley as garnish with lemon wedges on table.

Swordfish with Cannellini Beans

 Serves 4 / Preparation: 10 mins / Total cooking time: 15–20 mins

2 cloves garlic, crushed

4 cloves garlic, finely chopped

2 tablespoons fresh oregano leaves

2 fl oz (60 ml) extra virgin olive oil

4 x 6 oz (180 g) swordfish steaks, seasoned
    with pepper and salt

5 oz (150 g) pancetta, cut into thin strips

4 scallions (shallots), finely chopped

2 x 14 oz (400 g) cans cannellini beans,
    drained and rinsed

3 x 2 in (5 cm) fresh rosemary sprigs

5½ fl oz (160 ml) good-quality chicken stock

4 tablespoons flat-leaf parsley, chopped, plus
    extra for serving

1 lemon, cut into quarters

mixed salad leaves

Mix crushed garlic with 2 tablespoons of the olive oil and oregano in dish. Add swordfish and turn to coat. Leave to marinate at room temperature while making the beans.

Heat remaining 1 tablespoon olive oil in frying pan over medium heat, add the chopped garlic, pancetta and scallions and cook for 4–5 minutes, stirring until starting to colour. Add cannellini beans, rosemary and stock, and simmer for 5 minutes or until stock is almost absorbed. Remove and discard rosemary sprigs.

Place 1 cup of the bean mixture into a small bowl and mash roughly with a fork, then return to the pan with chopped parsley and stir through for 1–2 minutes. Remove pan from heat, cover and keep warm.

Heat char-grill over high heat and cook swordfish for 2 minutes each side, or until cooked but still pink in the centre.

Spoon braised bean mixture onto serving plates and top with fish, sprinkle with chopped parsley and serve with lemon wedges and mixed green salad.

Chorizo with Mixed Beans

Serves 4 / Preparation: 20 mins
/ Total cooking time: 1 hour 20 mins plus overnight soaking

3 ½ oz (100 g) each dried black eye, kidney
    and borlotti beans, soaked overnight
2 sprigs fresh thyme
4 bay leaves
sea salt
2½ fl oz (80 ml) olive oil
2 brown onions, thinly sliced
3 cloves garlic, thinly sliced
1 large carrot, cut into thick slices
1 leek (use white part only), thinly sliced
1½ tablespoons ground cumin

1 bunch cilantro (coriander), leaves
    separated, stems and roots finely chopped
1 cup (250 ml) dry white wine
1 x 14 oz (400 g) can chopped tomatoes
large pinch of saffron threads, soaked in 1
    cup hot water for 20 minutes
1 cup finely shredded cabbage
1 cup flat-leaf parsley, chopped
2 chorizo sausages (3½ oz/100 g each), sliced
    thinly on an angle
flat bread, lightly grilled

Rinse and drain the beans in cold water and place in a large saucepan with thyme sprigs, 2 bay leaves and salt. Fill pan with cold water to cover beans and bring to a simmer over medium heat. Cook beans for 30 minutes or until just tender. Drain, remove bay leaves and set aside.

Heat olive oil in a deep frying pan, add onions and garlic and fry over a moderate heat for 5 minutes, stirring until soft. Add drained beans, carrot, leek, cumin, chopped coriander stems and roots, and remaining 2 bay leaves. Cook for 8–10 minutes or until leek has softened. Add white wine and bring to the boil, then add tomatoes and saffron water. Simmer for 20 minutes, stirring, until most of the liquid has absorbed. Add cabbage and coriander leaves. Season with salt and pepper to taste, simmer for 5–10 minutes until cabbage wilts (do not overcook the cabbage, it still needs to be a little firm).

Meanwhile, heat a grill or frying pan over medium heat and cook chorizo for about 2 minutes each side. Remove and roll in paper towel to absorb excess oil.

Quickly brown flat bread on heated grill, about 1 minute each side.

Spoon bean mix onto serving platter and top with chorizo. Sprinkle with extra chopped coriander and serve with warm flat bread.

Braised Beans, Ricotta and Oregano with Tomato Sauce

Serves 4 / Preparation: 15 mins / Total cooking time: 30 mins

10½ oz (300 g) baby green beans, trimmed

10½ oz (300 g) roma beans, trimmed and cut
  into 4 in (10 cm) lengths

8 oz (220 g) firm ricotta, crumbled

TOMATO SAUCE

1¾ fl oz (50 ml) olive oil, plus extra

1 medium onion, finely chopped

2 cloves garlic, thinly sliced

1 teaspoon crushed chilli

1 tablespoon ground cumin

1 teaspoon cinnamon

2 teaspoons smoked paprika

2 cardamom pods, crushed

¼ cup fresh oregano

2 x 14 oz (400 g) cans tomatoes

2 tablespoons honey

ground black pepper and sea salt

Turkish bread, lightly toasted

To make the tomato sauce, heat oil in saucepan over medium–high heat, add onion, garlic and chilli and sauté for 7–8 minutes or until softened. Add spices and fresh oregano, cook for 1–2 minutes until fragrant, add canned tomatoes and simmer for 10–15 minutes or until mixture has thickened. Add honey, season with pepper and salt and keep warm.

Blanch beans for 2–3 minutes or until just tender. Drain and add to tomato sauce, stir to mix through. Transfer to serving bowl, gently fold through ricotta, season with pepper and salt to taste, drizzle over extra olive oil. Serve with warm Turkish bread.

Broad Bean and Fennel Tart

 Serves 4 / Preparation: 30 mins / Total cooking time: 50 mins

1 large shortcrust pastry sheet
2 tablespoons light olive oil
1 large fennel bulb, thinly sliced
4 oz (120 g) frozen broad beans, podded
3 large eggs, plus 1 egg yolk

9 oz (250 g) sour cream
⅓ cup parmesan cheese, grated
salt and pepper
mixed salad leaves for serving

Preheat the oven to 350°F (180°C) and grease a deep 9½ in (24-cm) loose-bottomed tart pan and line the pan with pastry. Trim pastry if overhanging. Prick with a fork and chill for 20 minutes. Cover pastry with baking paper, fill with pastry weights or uncooked rice. Place on oven tray and bake for 10 minutes. Remove paper and weights or rice, then bake for a further 5 minutes or until golden and cooked. Cool at room temperature. Place broad beans in a bowl of boiling water. When cool, remove the skins.

Meanwhile, heat the oil in a frying pan over a low–medium heat. Add fennel, season with salt and pepper and cook for 10 minutes, stirring occasionally until softened slightly.

Spread the fennel over the base of the tart case and scatter over broad beans.

Place eggs, plus extra yolk, sour cream and parmesan in a jug, season with salt and pepper and beat well with a fork until smooth. Pour into the tart shell, and return to oven on baking try and cook for 20–25 minutes until golden and set.

Remove from oven and rest for 5 minutes. Cut into 4 slices and serve with mixed green salad.

Broad Bean and Gruyère Risotto

Serves 6–8 / Preparation: 15 mins / Total cooking time: 25 mins

6 cups vegetable stock

9 oz (250 g) frozen broad beans

1 tablespoon extra virgin olive oil

1 small leek, thinly sliced

2 cups arborio rice

½ cup dry white wine

9 fl oz (200 g), gruyère cheese, coarsely grated

5 oz (150 g) thickened cream

2 cups arugula (rocket) leaves

⅓ cup pine nuts, lightly toasted

Pour stock into medium saucepan and bring to a simmer. Reduce heat to low.

Place frozen broad beans in a bowl of boiling water. When cool, remove the skins and set aside.

In a large, heavy-based saucepan, heat oil on medium heat. Sauté leek 3–4 minutes until soft. Add rice and coat with leek, cook for 1 minute, stirring constantly.

Pour wine into saucepan and cook until absorbed, about 1 minute. Add hot stock, one cup at a time, stirring until all liquid has been absorbed, about 15–20 minutes. Rice should be soft with a slight bite. Stir through broad beans.

Remove from heat. Add cheese, cream and gruyère and stir into rice. Season to taste. Cover and set aside for 2 minutes.

Spoon into serving bowls and sprinkle over toasted pine nuts.

Cannellini Bean and Coconut Curry

Serves 4 / Preparation: 10 mins / Total cooking time: 15 mins

2 tablespoons sunflower oil

1 teaspoon yellow mustard seeds

1 onion, thinly sliced

12 fresh curry leaves*

1.5 in (3 cm) piece ginger, peeled and grated

5 cloves garlic, finely chopped

3 teaspoons mild curry powder

4 cardamom pods, lightly bruised

½ teaspoon ground turmeric

½ teaspoon chilli powder

1 teaspoon ground coriander

6 fl oz (185 ml) coconut milk

2 x 14 oz (400 g) cans cannellini beans, rinsed and drained

9 oz (250 g) grape or cherry tomatoes, cut in half

9 oz (250g) butternut pumpkin, cut into small pieces

2 teaspoons sugar

juice of 1 lime

3 tablespoons chopped cilantro (coriander) leaves, plus extra for garnish

basmati rice

naan bread

Heat the oil in a large-sized saucepan over low–medium heat. Add mustard seeds and cook for 30 seconds or until they start to pop. Add onion and curry leaves, stir 4–5 minutes until soft. Add ginger, garlic, curry powder and spices, cook stirring, for about 2 minutes until fragrant.

Add the coconut milk and 7 fl oz (200 ml) water, bring to a simmer. Reduce heat to low and simmer for a further 4–5 minutes until mixture has thickened slightly. Add beans, tomatoes, pumpkin, sugar and lime juice, simmer for a further 2–3 minutes until tomatoes have become a little soft. Gently fold through chopped cilantro. Serve with rice and naan bread and finish off with the extra cilantro.

*Curry leaves are available from selected greengrocers.

Couscous and Cannellini Bean Burgers

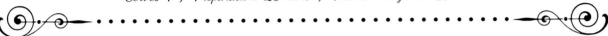

2½ fl oz (80 ml) vegetable stock

3½ oz (100 g) couscous

3 tablespoons extra virgin olive oil

½ red onion, finely chopped

3 cloves garlic, crushed

1 tablespoon crushed chilli

1 x 14 oz (400 g) can cannellini beans, rinsed
    and drained

2 tablespoons mint, finely chopped

3 teaspoons lemon zest, grated finely

1 Turkish loaf, split in half lengthways and
    cut into 4 pieces, toasted

7 oz (200 g) hummus

arugula (rocket), to serve

1 tomato, sliced

1 small can pineapple rings

1 small can beetroot

natural yoghurt, for serving

Pour stock into small saucepan and bring to the boil. Place couscous in a heatproof bowl, pour over stock and stir. Cover with cling wrap and set aside for 5 minutes. Remove cling wrap and fluff couscous with a fork.

Heat 1 tablespoon of olive oil in small frying pan over medium heat. Cook the onion for 2–3 minutes until soft. Add the garlic and crushed chilli, cook until fragrant, about 2 minutes.

Place the beans in a food processor, add the onion mix, mint and lemon zest. Pulse until mixture combines together. Place mixture in couscous bowl and fold through. Season with salt and pepper to taste, form into four patties, cover and chill for 30 minutes.

Heat the remaining 2 tablespoons oil in frying pan over medium heat and cook patties for 2 minutes each side. Remove from pan and drain on paper towel.

Meanwhile, toast bread and spread one side of each slice with hummus, top four of the slices with some arugula, pineapple, beetroot, a patty and a dollop of yoghurt each. Top with the remaining bread.

Mini Thyme Bean Cakes

Serves 6 / Preparation: 15 mins / Total cooking time: 25 mins

1 x 400 g (14 oz) can borlotti beans
2 scallions (shallots), thinly sliced
½ cup thickened cream
1 egg, beaten
2 sprigs thyme, leaves removed or
    ½ teaspoon dried thyme

1 teaspoon chopped parsley or 1 teaspoon
    dried parsley
½ teaspoon black pepper
pinch of salt

Preheat the oven to 400°F (200°C). Grease a mini-muffin tin.

Drain beans, rinse and place in a blender.

Add sliced shallots, cream, egg, thyme, parsley and black pepper and salt. Blend until roughly mixed.

Scoop two teaspoons into each mini-muffin tin slot. Bake for 10 minutes or until brown on top.

You can dish up these delicious treats any time—for an afternoon snack, at a party or take them to a picnic.

Spicy Bean Patties with Red Quinoa

Serves 4

½ cup red quinoa (any colour quinoa can be used)

1 cup water

1 x 14 oz (400 g) can butter beans

1 x 14 oz (400 g) can kidney beans

2 teaspoons crushed garlic

5 scallions (shallots), finely chopped

1 teaspoon ground cumin

1 teaspoon chilli powder (or one fresh red chilli, chopped)

3 tablespoons roughly chopped cilantro (coriander)

1 egg, beaten

¼ teaspoon sea salt

¼ teaspoon ground black pepper

2 tablespoons olive oil

Rinse the quinoa in a fine colander and place in a small saucepan with the water. Bring to the boil, reduce heat, cover and simmer for 8 minutes or until all the water is absorbed. Remove from the heat and set aside to cool.

Rinse and drain the beans and coarsely mash with a potato masher or a large fork and place in a bowl. Add the cooked quinoa, garlic, scallions, cumin, chilli, coriander, egg and salt and pepper. Mix until all the ingredients are well combined. Divide the mixture into round patties.

Place the patties, covered, in the fridge for approximately 1 hour.

Heat the olive oil in a non-stick frying pan over medium heat. Add the patties and cook until golden on both sides, approximately 3–4 minutes each side depending on how hot you have the pan.

These patties are delicious for lunch or dinner. You can sandwich them in between bread for a bean burger, roll them in a wrap or serve with fresh salad or vegetables.

This recipe is courtesy of a friend of mine, and a successful cookbook author in her own right, Rena Patten. We love making this recipe of hers, from her cookbook, 'Cooking with Quinoa'. We make it all the time and have tweaked it a little.

SIDES

Baby Green Beans with Asparagus

9 oz (250 g) baby green beans, trimmed

2 bunches asparagus, ends removed,
    trimmed and halved on the diagonal

DRESSING

¼ cup tahini

2 tablespoons tamari sauce

1 tablespoon superfine (caster) sugar

1 tablespoon rice wine vinegar

1 teaspoon fresh ginger, finely chopped

1 tablespoon warm water

3 scallions (shallots), sliced diagonally

Steam beans and asparagus for about 3 minutes until just tender, drain and refresh in cold water.

In a small mixing bowl add tahini, tamari sauce, sugar, vinegar, ginger and water and mix until sugar has dissolved.

Place vegetables into serving bowl and drizzle over dressing and top with scallions.

Broad Beans, Goat's Cheese and Fresh Herbs

Serves 6 / Preparation time: 10 mins / Soaking: 5 mins

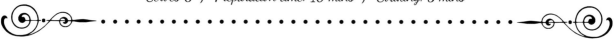

1 lb (500 g) frozen broad beans, podded

2 tablespoons virgin olive oil

1 tablespoon white wine vinegar

1 scallion (shallot), chopped

1 tablespoon chives, chopped

1 tablespoon parsley, chopped

1 tablespoon mint, chopped

1¾ oz (50 g) goat's cheese

Place broad beans in a large heatproof bowl. Pour over boiling water to cover. Set aside for 5 minutes to soak. Peel and discard skins.

Mix together oil, vinegar and scallion in a bowl. Add peeled broad beans and toss to coat. Transfer the mixture to a large shallow serving bowl. Scatter chives, parsley, mint and goat's cheese over the top.

Greek Butter Beans with Arugula

Serves 4 / Preparation: 10 mins / Cooking time: 25 mins

1 tablespoon olive oil

1 large red onion, cut into thin wedges

3 cloves garlic, thinly sliced

1 x 24 oz (690 g) jar tomato puree (passata)

4 vine-ripened tomatoes, peeled and
  chopped

2 x 14 oz (400 g) cans butter beans, rinsed
  and drained

½ cup flat-leaf parsley, chopped

2 tablespoons fresh oregano leaves, chopped

1¾ oz (50 g) arugula (rocket leaves)

⅓ cup shaved parmesan cheese

Heat oil in a large deep saucepan over medium heat. Add red onion and garlic. Cook, stirring often, for about 3 minutes. Add tomato puree, tomatoes, butter beans and fresh herbs. Cover and bring to the boil. Reduce heat and simmer for about 10 minutes. Uncover and cook for a further 10 minutes or until sauce thickens.

Just before you serve, toss through arugula and sprinkle with cheese.

If you want to turn this hearty side into a filling main meal, serve it with some quinoa, rice or risoni.

Green Beans, Capers and Roasted Almonds

Serves 4–6 / Preparation: 30 mins / Total cooking time: 30 mins

16 oz (480 g) baby green beans, trimmed

2 tablespoons extra virgin olive oil

4 scallions (shallots), thinly sliced

3 teaspoons baby capers, rinsed

1/3 cup slivered almonds, roasted

2 tablespoons finely chopped flat-leaf parsley

sea salt and freshly ground black pepper

Cook beans in boiling salted water until just tender but firm to the bite. Drain, refresh in iced water and drain again.

Heat the olive oil in a heavy-based frying pan, add scallions and cook over low heat for 8 minutes or until soft. Add capers and cook for another 2 minutes, then add beans and season to taste with sea salt and freshly ground pepper. Stir for another 5 minutes or until beans are heated through. Add almonds and parsley, combine well and serve immediately.

This is lovely with grilled steak, fish or chicken

Green Beans Gratin

Serves 4 / Preparation: 10 mins / Total cooking time: 4 mins

1 tablespoon light cooking oil
1 clove garlic, crushed
1 teaspoon ginger, freshly grated
1 teaspoon freshly chopped cilantro
  (coriander)

½ teaspoon cumin
½ teaspoon garam masala
2 vine-ripened tomatoes, diced
20 long green beans, cut in half diagonally
1 teaspoon mint, chopped

Heat the oil in a frying pan over a medium–high heat. Add garlic, ginger, cilantro, cumin and garam masala. Cook for ½ minute. Add tomatoes and cook for ½ minute. Add beans and cook for about 3 minutes or until just tender. Stir in 1 tablespoon of the chopped fresh mint to serve.

Runner Beans and Snow Peas with Mustard Dressing

Serves 6 / Preparation: 5 mins / Total cooking time: 5 mins

¼ cup extra virgin olive oil

juice of 1 medium lemon

2 teaspoons seeded mustard

1 clove garlic, crushed

10½ oz (300 g) runner beans

6 oz (180 g) snow peas, washed and sliced in
 half

¼ cup fresh chives, finely chopped

Mix oil, lemon juice, mustard and garlic together in small bowl. Season to taste.

Steam beans and snow peas for about 3 minutes or until just tender. Toss vegetables in oil and lemon juice mixture to coat.

Transfer to a serving bowl and scatter with chopped chives.

DESSERTS

Baked Ricotta with Cherries in Vanilla Syrup

Serves 8 / Preparation: 50 mins / Total cooking time: 50 mins

BAKED RICOTTA

24 oz (750 g) ricotta

2 free-range eggs

1 vanilla bean, split and seeds scraped

6 oz (175 g) superfine (caster) sugar

7 oz (200 g) unsalted pistachio kernels

CHERRIES IN VANILLA SYRUP

10 oz (280 g) superfine (caster) sugar

1 lemon

3½ fl oz (100 ml) cold water

leftover vanilla pod from baked ricotta

2 fl oz (55 ml) kirsch*

9 oz (250 g) fresh cherries

BAKED RICOTTA

Preheat the oven to 300°F (150°C).

Beat ricotta and eggs together in a large bowl, fold in only seeds from the vanilla bean. Add sugar and nuts and beat well. Spoon ricotta mixture into a non-stick loaf tin, 8 x 4 in (21 x 10 cm), and smooth the top, then cover with foil.

Place the loaf tin in a roasting pan and pour in enough boiling water to come halfway up the outside of the loaf tin. Bake until firm, about 50 minutes. Remove from the water, take off foil and cool completely in fridge for at least 3 hours before turning out onto a plate to serve.

CHERRIES IN VANILLA SYRUP

Put sugar, a small piece of the lemon rind, and the vanilla pod in a saucepan and cook over a medium heat for 10 minutes or until the mixture has turned a pale caramel. Remove from heat and add a squeeze of lemon juice and the kirsch to stop the cooking process. Cool completely but don't refrigerate—about 45 minutes.

Working over a bowl, remove cherry stems and tear the cherries in half removing the stone. Keep refrigerated until ready to serve.

To serve, slice the ricotta into 8 pieces. Remove lemon rind and vanilla pod from the syrup, then pour over the cherries. Spoon the cherry mixture over the ricotta.

*Kirsch is unsweetened cherry brandy available from bottle shops

Ricotta and cherry mixture can be made up to 2 days in advance and kept in refrigerator. Other stone fruits can be used when in season to replace cherries. Other varieties of nuts can be used in ricotta.

Bread and Butter Pudding

2½ oz (85 g) craisins

2 ½ fl oz (80 ml) port, warmed

32 fl oz (900 ml) pure thin cream

1 vanilla bean, split and seeds scraped

12 egg yolks

5½ oz (165 g) superfine (caster) sugar

12 slices stale thick white bread, crusts removed

½ loaf white Turkish bread, cut into 8 bread size slices

2 oz (65 g) softened unsalted butter

confectioner's (icing) sugar, to dust

thick cream, to serve

Preheat the oven to 320°F (160°C). Butter a 4-cup baking dish. Combine the craisins and port in a small bowl and leave to macerate for 5 minutes.

Place cream, vanilla pod and seeds in a saucepan over medium heat. Bring to just below boiling point, then set aside to infuse while preparing the custard.

Place egg yolks and sugar in a bowl, whisk with a balloon whisk until combined.

Remove and discard vanilla pod from the cream, then pour the hot cream over the cold egg mixture, whisking to combine.

Spread the bread with the softened unsalted butter, then halve diagonally. Layer one-third of the bread in the dish, overlapping slightly. Sprinkle with one-third of the craisins and ladle over just enough of the custard to cover. Leave to soak for 20 minutes, then repeat with the remaining bread and custard mixture twice more, finishing with Turkish bread as top layer, giving a crunchy topping effect when cooked. Soak for a further 2 hours before cooking.

Place the dish in a baking pan. Fill the pan with just enough boiling water to come halfway up the sides of the dish. Bake for 45–55 minutes until golden and just set. If top is browning too quickly, cover loosely with foil. Dust pudding with sifted icing sugar and serve with thick cream.

Baked Vanilla Fruits with Coconut Custard

Serves 4–6 / Preparation: 15 mins / Total cooking time: 50 mins

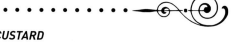

4 nectarines (mix of yellow and white)

4 peaches (mix of yellow and white)

11 oz (330 g) superfine (caster) sugar

1 vanilla bean and split, seeds scraped

2 cups water

COCONUT CUSTARD

14 fl oz (400 ml) can coconut cream

10½ fl oz (300 ml) full cream milk

1 teaspoon vanilla extract

6 medium egg yolks

3½ oz (110 g) superfine (caster) sugar

2 teaspoons cornstarch (cornflour), sifted

pinch of salt

Preheat the oven to 340°F (170°C).

Place the nectarines and peaches into a deep ceramic baking dish.

Place the sugar, vanilla bean and seeds, and the water in a saucepan and bring to the boil over medium heat, stirring until sugar has dissolved. Remove from heat and pour the sugar syrup over nectarines and peaches. Transfer to the oven and bake for 25 minutes or until fruit is tender.

COCONUT CUSTARD

Place the coconut cream, milk and vanilla extract in a saucepan over medium heat and cook for 4–5 minutes, stirring, until just below boiling point.

Meanwhile, place the egg yolks, sugar, sifted cornstarch and a pinch of salt in a bowl. Using electric beaters, beat for 3–4 minutes or until the mixture is thick and pale. Gradually beat in the coconut cream mixture, then place in a clean pan over low heat. Cook, stirring constantly with a wooden spoon, for 10 minutes or until the custard is thick enough to coat the back of the spoon.

Serve warm fruit with coconut custard.

Fruit can also be served chilled with warm custard.

Blackberry and Raspberry Lemon Syrup Cake

9 oz (250 g) softened unsalted butter

1 lb (500 g) superfine (caster) sugar

½ tsp vanilla bean extract

6 free-range eggs

12 oz (340 g) all-purpose (plain) flour

2 oz (60 g) desiccated coconut

2 oz (60 g) shredded coconut

2 teaspoons baking powder

5 fl oz (140 ml) coconut milk

5 fl oz (140 ml) full cream milk

zest of 1 lemon

9 oz (250 g) blackberries

9 oz (250 g) raspberries

thickened cream, to serve

LEMON SYRUP

6 fl oz (180 ml) lemon juice

6 oz (180 g) superfine (caster) sugar

finely grated zest of 2 lemons

1½ oz (40 g) toasted shredded coconut

Preheat the oven to 350°F (180°C). Grease and line a 11 in (26 cm) round cake tin

Beat butter and sugar in an electric mixer until pale and creamy, add vanilla extract, then eggs one at a time, scraping down bowl after each addition.

Combine flour, both coconuts and baking powder in a large bowl. Combine coconut milk and full cream milk in a jug, then stir flour mixture and milk mixture in alternate batches into butter mixture, finishing with flour mixture. Stir through lemon zest.

Pour into the cake tin and bake for 45–55 minutes. Cake should be golden and spring back when pressed with fingertips. Prick a few holes in the cake with a skewer.

To make the lemon syrup, stir the lemon juice and sugar in a small saucepan over low heat until sugar has dissolved, set aside to cool, then add lemon rind.

Before serving, pour half of the lemon syrup into a jug, add blackberries and raspberries and pour over cake. Top with toasted shredded coconut to serve.

Put remainder of lemon syrup into a small serving jug and pour over cake once plated. Serve with a dollop of thickened cream.

Coffee Bean and Raspberry Ice-cream

Serves 6–8 / Preparation: 40 mins
/ Total cooling time: 3 hours plus freezing time

13 fl oz (375 ml) full cream milk

6 oz (170 g) superfine (caster) sugar

1½ cups whole coffee beans

pinch of salt

13 fl oz (375 ml) thickened cream

5 large egg yolks

1 cup frozen blended raspberries

¼ teaspoon vanilla extract

¼ teaspoon coffee (finely ground, press
 grinds through a fine mesh sieve)

Heat milk, sugar, whole coffee beans, salt and ½ cup of the cream in a medium saucepan until warm and steamy. Do not boil. Remove from the heat, cover and leave to sit at room temperature for 1 hour.

Pour the remaining 1 cup of cream into a medium metal bowl, sit on ice over a larger bowl. Place a mesh strainer on top of the bowls and set aside.

Reheat the milk and coffee mixture over medium heat until hot and steamy (not boiling). In a separate bowl, whisk the egg yolks, slowly pour the heated milk and coffee mixture into the egg yolks, whisking constantly so that the yolks are tempered by the warm milk, but not cooked. Scrape the warmed egg yolks back into the saucepan.

Stir the mixture constantly over medium heat with a flat-bottomed spatula, scraping the bottom while stirring until the mixture thickens and coats the spatula so that you can run your finger across the coating and have the coating not run. This should take about 10 minutes.

Pour the custard through the strainer and stir it into the cream. Press on the coffee beans in the strainer to extract as much of the coffee flavour as possible. Discard the coffee beans. Add vanilla extract and finely ground coffee, stir until cool.

Chill the mixture thoroughly. Blend frozen raspberries and fold through mixture then freeze it in your ice-cream maker as per the instructions.

Serve with wafer biscuits and/or fresh raspberries.

Grilled Apricots with Cinnamon Cream

3½ oz (100 g) natural yoghurt

½ teaspoon ground cinnamon

1 teaspoon vanilla bean paste

1 tablespoon superfine (caster) sugar

7 fl oz (200 ml) thickened cream, whipped

12 medium-sized apricots, halved, stones
  removed

raw sugar, for sprinkling

Combine yoghurt, cinnamon, vanilla bean paste and sugar into a medium bowl and fold through whipped cream. Cover with plastic wrap and refrigerate until ready to serve (cinnamon cream can be made day before).

Preheat the grill.

Place apricot halves, cut side up, on a baking tray lined with baking paper. Sprinkle with raw sugar. Cook under the grill for 8 minutes or until apricots are soft and sugar has melted.

Arrange on platter with cinnamon cream.

Macerated Peaches with Sorbet

Serves 6 / Preparation: 15 mins
/ Total cooking time: 15 mins plus cooling, refrigeration and freezing time

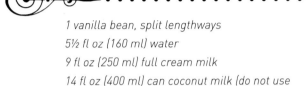

1 vanilla bean, split lengthways

5½ fl oz (160 ml) water

9 fl oz (250 ml) full cream milk

14 fl oz (400 ml) can coconut milk (do not use
 light milk)

1 tablespoon brandy

10 medium-sized (yellow) peaches, stones
 removed

2 tablespoons brown sugar

2½ fl oz (80 ml) freshly squeezed orange juice

Combine caster sugar, vanilla bean and water in saucepan. Stir over low heat until sugar has dissolved, then bring to the boil, simmer for 10 minutes. Discard the vanilla bean and pour syrup into a medium bowl. Reserve.

Pour the milk and coconut milk into the same saucepan and heat until just warm. Remove pan from heat and stir in the reserved syrup, add brandy and cool at room temperature.

Churn the mixture in an ice-cream machine or pour into a shallow container, place it in the freezer, stirring hourly until sorbet freezes.

Cut the peaches into thick slices into a bowl. Add brown sugar and orange juice and toss until peaches are well coated. Cover with plastic wrap and refrigerate for 1 hour.

To serve, divide the peaches into 6 glass serving bowls and spoon over coconut sorbet.

Peach, Raspberry and Ricotta Cake

Serves 6–8 / Preparation: 30 mins / Total cooking time: 1¼ hours

8 oz (220 g) sour cream

1 teaspoon baking soda (bicarbonate of soda)

10½ oz (300 g) all-purpose (plain) flour

8 oz (220 g) superfine (caster) sugar

5½ oz (160 g) softened unsalted butter

1 oz (30 g) almond meal

2 limes, zested

½ teaspoon vanilla bean paste

1 teaspoon baking powder

½ teaspoon sea salt

2 medium-sized eggs

3 ripe peaches skin on, halved and thinly sliced

4 oz (125 g) raspberries, plus extra for serving (can use frozen berries, thaw before using)

7 oz (200 g) firm ricotta, crumbled coarsely confectioners' (icing) sugar sieved, dust for serving

1 x 4 fl oz (125 ml) Greek yoghurt, for serving

Grease and line a 8 in (20 cm) square cake tin.

Mix sour cream and bicarbonate of soda in a jug and leave for 2–3 minutes to foam (mixture will increase in volume).

Preheat the oven to 350°F (180°C). Pulse flour, sugar, butter, almond meal, lime zest, vanilla bean paste, baking powder and salt in food processor until mixture becomes crumbly. Set aside 1 cup of the crumb mix into a small bowl.

Add eggs and sour cream mixture to food processor, pulse until just smooth, then spread half the mix in the base of the cake tin buttered and lined with baking paper. Scatter with half the peaches, half the raspberries, half the ricotta and one-third of the reserved crumb mixture. Spread remaining sour cream mixture over and smooth top. Scatter with remaining peaches, raspberries, ricotta and reserved crumb mixture. Bake until golden (skewer should come out clean when cooked through) for 1–1¼ hours (cover with foil if cake is browning too much).

Set cake aside to cool in the tin for about 15 minutes, then turn onto wire rack to cool. Dust with confectioners' sugar.

Serve with Greek yoghurt for a healthy alternative to cream.

Cake will keep for 2 days in airtight container.

Ricotta Tart with Blueberries

2 sheets shortcrust pastry

9 oz (250 g) fresh ricotta

3½ oz (110 g) superfine (caster) sugar

3 eggs

1 teaspoon vanilla bean paste

4 fl oz (125 ml) thickened cream

2 tablespoons all-purpose (plain) flour

grated zest of 1 lemon, plus 2 tablespoons
     lemon juice

BLUEBERRY COMPOTE

9 oz (250 g) blueberries

1 vanilla bean, split and seeds scraped

3½ oz (110 g) superfine (caster) sugar

2 teaspoons arrowroot

Preheat the oven to 350°F (180°C).

Line the pastry in a rectangular loose-bottomed 13 x 4 in (34 x 10 cm) buttered tart pan. Trim the pastry to fit the pan and carefully place the pastry inside the tart pan, pressing the pastry around the edges. Prick the base with a fork and line with baking paper. Fill with pastry weights or uncooked rice, bake for 10 minutes, then remove paper and weights. Bake for 3 minutes until golden.

Blend remaining ingredients in a food processor until smooth. Pour into the tart case and bake for 30 minutes until set. Cool.

BLUEBERRY COMPOTE

Place blueberries, vanilla pod and seeds and sugar in a small saucepan with 4 fl oz (125 ml) water and stir over low heat until sugar has dissolved. Simmer for 3 minutes. Mix arrowroot with 2 tablespoons each water and berry liquid. Stir into berries and cook for 2 minutes until thickened. Cool.

Top tart with compote and serve.

Vanilla Biscuits

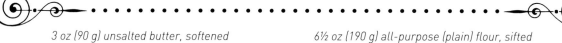

Makes about 30 / Preparation: 25 mins / Total cooking time: 12 mins

3 oz (90 g) unsalted butter, softened

1 oz (30 g) vegetable shortening (cold)

8 oz (225 g) superfine (caster) sugar

2 vanilla beans, cut in half lengthways,
    seeds scraped

1 egg

1 teaspoon vanilla extract

6½ oz (190 g) all-purpose (plain) flour, sifted

1 teaspoon baking powder

½ teaspoon salt

1 teaspoon cinnamon

¼ teaspoon superfine (caster) sugar

Beat together butter, shortening and ¾ cup sugar in electric mixer until light and fluffy. Add vanilla bean seeds, egg and vanilla extract and beat until combined well. Add sifted flour, baking powder and salt into mixture until just combined.

Form dough into a 8 x 2 in (20 x 5 cm) log on a sheet of baking paper, roll up in cling wrap, then foil and refrigerate for at least 4 hours or overnight.

Preheat the oven to 350°F (180°C).

Remove cling wrap and foil, roll log in remaining ½ cup sugar and cinnamon on a sheet of baking paper (not all sugar will stick to the log). Mix the rest of the sugar and the cinnamon together on a plate. Cut log crosswise into ¼ in (½ cm) thick slices and dip cut sides of slices in sugar and cinnamon mix.

Arrange biscuits about 1 in (2.5 cm) apart on a tray lined with baking paper. Cook in batches for about 10–12 minutes, or until edges are light golden in colour. Transfer cooked biscuits with metal spatula to a wire rack to cool.

Vanilla bean can be used at a later date. Uncooked dough keeps refrigerated for up to three days wrapped in cling wrap and foil. Cooked biscuits will keep in an airtight container for five days.

Vanilla Bean Custard

Serves 4 / Preparation: 20 mins / Total cooking time: 10 minutes

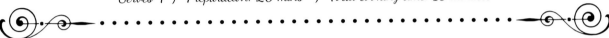

10½ fl oz (300 ml) pure cream (thin)

1¾ fl oz (50 ml) full-cream milk

1 vanilla bean, split lengthways, seeds
    scraped

6 medium egg yolks at room temperature

2½ oz (75 g) superfine (caster) sugar

Heat the cream, milk, vanilla pod and seeds in heavy-based saucepan over medium heat until just below boiling point, then remove from heat. Meanwhile, use a whisk to mix the egg yolks and sugar in a bowl until well combined. Gradually whisk hot milk mixture into egg yolk mixture, then pour back into the same saucepan and return to a medium-low heat.

Using a wooden spoon, stir continuously, gently making sure you reach the base and edges of the saucepan for 4–5 minutes until the custard is 170°F (75°C) on a sugar thermometer and is thick enough to coat the back of a spoon.

Remove from heat and strain through a fine sieve into a clean bowl, discarding the vanilla pod. Cool for 15 minutes, stirring occasionally, then cover the surface with cling wrap to prevent a skin from forming and cool completely in fridge.

This can be served cold or hot. Serve with cake, fruit or on its own.

Sugar thermometers are available from kitchenware shops.

ACKNOWLEDGEMENTS

Where do I start, so many people, so many bean stories. I kept seeing bean recipes in every magazine and thinking that would make a great cookbook. I was visiting with Di and we both got enthused about creating our own bean cookbook. So we proceeded to go through hundreds of recipes from magazines and cookbooks, adding our own personal variations.

The next step was months of cooking each recipe—we didn't realise what we had taken on. But, in saying that, it was so much fun.

Thanks to my wonderful Mum, who is in her eighties, whose well-honed cooking skills and willingness to give anything a go, has been a fantastic help with the recipe testing. And thanks to Dad, in his nineties, who is a good taste-tester. To the rest of my family, thanks for supporting most of my crazy ideas.

To my loving, supportive hubby Peter—I would never try to do all these things without your support. He is a great sounding board for culinary challenges.

New Holland Publishers and Fiona Schultz especially and her magic team changed my life eight years ago when they suggested I be a publishing agent for New Holland and I am still loving the support they give to me and am amazed when I look at my book shelf and see all the people I have met and all the cookbooks and biographies we have produced together. Also, seeing they make such beautiful books I knew it would be a great adventure to actually go on myself.

Linda

As Linda mentioned, this started off very innocently and here we are authors of a cookbook. As a mother of two girls, Katie and Sally, I have had to slip vegetables by them in many ways and forms so have been cooking for many years with an eye out for tasty, healthy and easy-to-prepare recipes and have not had too many complaints. I love having dinner parties as food brings people together and I am an avid conversationalist, so thank you to all my friends who have come along on the journey of my culinary experiences. Thank you to my daughters for your support. Linda, for suggesting we collaborate—we've had such fun. To my extended family thank you for just being there. New Holland Publishers for taking on the challenge and all your hard work helping make this a beautiful cook book.

Di

Index